Meetings with Mrs. Collins

Sketches of Life and Events on Montana's Open Range; from the Diaries of Frontier Photographer Evelyn Cameron, 1893-1907

Colleen Elizabeth Carter

**Outskirts Press, Inc.
Denver, Colorado**

The opinions expressed in this manuscript are solely the opinions of the author and do not represent the opinions or thoughts of the publisher. The author represents and warrants that s/he either owns or has the legal right to publish all material in this book.

Meetings with Mrs. Collins:
Sketches of Life and Events on Montana's Open Range; from the Diaries of Frontier Photographer Evelyn Cameron, 1893-1907
All Rights Reserved.
Copyright © 2008 Colleen Elizabeth Carter
V4.0

Front cover photo: "Evelyn on Jim," *Cameron photograph, courtesy of the Prairie County Museum, Terry, Montana (Box XVII, Neg. 3, EC3)* All rights reserved - used with permission.

This book may not be reproduced, transmitted, or stored in whole or in part by any means, including graphic, electronic, or mechanical without written permission except in the case of brief quotations embodied in critical articles and reviews.

Outskirts Press, Inc.
http://www.outskirtspress.com

PB ISBN: 978-1-4327-2709-3
HB ISBN: 978-1-4327-2925-7

Library of Congress Control Number: 2008930516

Outskirts Press and the "OP" logo are trademarks belonging to Outskirts Press, Inc.

PRINTED IN THE UNITED STATES OF AMERICA

Table of Contents

Acknowledgements vii
Introduction ix
Chapter 1: *"Mrs. Collins knows all about everybody."* 1
Chapter 2: *"Mrs. C. talked all day, amusing to me to hear her."* ... 11
Chapter 3: *"Curious little building, narrow and high."* 15
Chapter 4: *"Great agony displayed was heartrending."* 23
Chapter 5: *"I pity poor old Mrs. Collins in her tents in this
  sort of weather."* 29
Chapter 6: *"She is such a rum 'un."* 33
Chapter 7: *"Mrs. Collins gone to Fallon yesterday & is
  going to live in tents."* 39
Chapter 8: *"Drew caught his wife in an indecent way
  in Miles City."* 49
Chapter 9: *"Ewen & I had a 'difference.'"* 53
Chapter 10: *"She gave me her family tree & experiences
  generally after leaving old Oireland."* 57
Chapter 11: *"I saw the dead wee thing laid out with
  white flowers on its little white coffin."* 77
Chapter 12: *"Mrs. Collins never drank now . . . unless she
  got into the blues."* 87
Chapter 13: *"She says she will go to Klondike with me &
  we are to keep an hotel."* 93
Chapter 14: *"She is a dear old body, I think."* 97
Chapter 15: *"She has got rail road men boarding with
  her at $3.75 a week."* 103

Chapter 16: *"Mrs. Collins has bought the Anderson house and the Jordon barn from Jordan."* 109
Chapter 17: *"First business day in Terry but got no customers!"* 111
Chapter 18: *"Mrs. Ingersoll just lost 16 month old baby."* 117
Chapter 19: *"Photographed Mrs. Collins."* 119
Chapter 20: *"She couldn't find her gown & lost her false teeth."* 127
Chapter 21: *"Off at last . . . Goodbyes to friends."* 131
Chapter 22: *"General Miles hitched onto our train in a private car."* 135
Chapter 23: *"Mrs. Collins hove in sight 11.20"* 139
Chapter 24: *"Mrs. Collins asked me to stay so did."* 149
Chapter 25: Changing Times 153
Conclusion 163
References...167
About the Author 173

To the "Collins Girls"

Marian
Marjorie
Jean
Kathleen

Acknowledgements

The writing of this book is mingled with many memories of my trips to Montana, accompanied by my loving partner William Cull, who has been indispensable and encouraging in all stages of this project.

I am especially indebted to Donna Lucey, whose book *Photographing Montana* has inspired my efforts and provided much background information for the story of Mary Collins and her friendship with Evelyn Cameron. Donna was kind enough to read an early draft of this book for historical accuracy, and has granted me permission to use quotations from *Photographing Montana*.

I would never have known about the Cameron diaries were it not for happening upon Peter Fish's *Sunset* article, "Lady with a Camera." Karen Stevenson's portrayal of "Lady Cameron" on stages throughout Montana has helped bring the eccentric Mrs. Collins to life.

For help in obtaining photographs and documents and answering my many questions, I would like to thank the wonderful volunteers of the Prairie County Museum: Mary Haughian, Wynona Breen, Ruth Franks, Gary and Carol Larson (special thanks to Carol Larson for granting me permission to visit and photograph the old Cameron ranch near Terry); the staff of the Prairie County Courthouse in Terry, Montana; the staffs of the Montana Historical Society Archives (in particular librarian Brian Shovers) and the Photograph Archives, in Helena, Montana; the Miles City Public Library; and the Miles City Schools District Office.

I would like to thank LeeAnne Krusemark, guest adjunct professor of writing and publishing, whose critique of my manuscript helped me realize the value of Mary Collins' story, and gave me hope that I could do justice to it. Thanks also to the encouragement of Tamanika Brock James, my author representative at Outskirts Press, who has helped me through the process of publication. Special thanks to Sandra Bendayan and James Leahy, who read the manuscript at various stages, helping with both content and editing, and who encouraged me with their enthusiasm for my project.

Jan Ingersoll, of Anchorage, Alaska, shared information about Lynn Ingersoll and his family.

My brother and niece, Jon and Jonna Carter, met us in Montana in 2003 and assisted in researching the Cameron diaries. My cousins Vicki Warzenski and Francine Kane drove from Minnesota to meet us in Terry for the 2005 premier of the film *Evelyn Cameron: Pictures from a Worthy Life*.

I greatly appreciate the Mendocino County Bookmobile and Interlibrary Loan services; also the LDS Family History Library volunteers in Ukiah, California, who helped locate census information. I could not have succeeded without some of Covelo's most valuable resources: June Marie's Gifts (copies and fax), The Round Valley Public Library (books and wi-fi connection), and John Marshall (technological support).

Lastly, I want to express my gratitude to Evelyn Cameron, whose preoccupation with the details of her life, and the urge to record them, have left us with a priceless document of frontier history.

Introduction

TERRY, MONTANA
TUESDAY, MARCH 20, 1900.

At twelve thirty on a cloudless spring day, a horse and rider entered the small town of Terry, Montana. They headed down a muddy street to Laundre Avenue, the thoroughfare that ran along the Northern Pacific Railroad tracks. The rider was a woman, whose long split skirt allowed her to sit astride her horse, in a style which had so recently scandalized the citizens of Miles City.

She carried a large, heavy box, fastened to her waist; a gun scabbard was lashed to the back of her saddle. She alighted before an old wood-frame building, a former store, now home to Mrs. Collins, one of Terry's oldest and most colorful residents.

Mrs. Collins welcomed her friend, Evelyn Cameron. She could see from the presence of the box and scabbard that Evelyn had, as promised, come to photograph her. From the gun scabbard, Evelyn pulled a tripod and quickly assembled it. To the tripod she fitted the box, a No. 5 Kodet camera. While looking on, Mrs. Collins confessed, in her thick Irish brogue, that she had not only misplaced her gown, but that she had also lost her false teeth.

For nearly a year, Evelyn had been determined to photograph her eccentric friend, but Mrs. Collins had proved to be one of her more challenging subjects. The first attempt, in September 1899, had required much fussing over which of her possessions would appear in the photograph. When Evelyn showed her the prints a few days later, Mrs. Collins had judged them "very good," but not acceptable—she felt that her dress was too short. Evelyn had promised her that she would try again in the spring, after she and her husband Ewen returned from their winter hunting trip in the badlands north of the Yellowstone River.

Now that day had arrived, and the job of photographing Mrs. Collins was taking an amusing turn:

> Mrs. Collins had [a] great time getting herself and [her] room ready. She couldn't find her gown & lost her false teeth. She thought her dog had gone off with them. Finally she wished me to go & borrow Mrs. Van Horn's, which I did. She had to take them out & wash them first!! Then they proved too large for her mouth. I found hers under [the] bed coverlid. Took 2 of her: 3 seconds, No. 4 diaphragm.

That night Evelyn recorded the story in her diary. No matter how exhausted, she rarely neglected the nightly task of filling her small leather-bound journal with the details of her busy life: of cooking, clothes-washing, ranching chores, photography, and gardening, as well as concerns for her husband Ewen's health, and their financially precarious life in Montana.

* * *

My fascination with Mary Collins, my great-great-grandmother, has its roots in childhood memories of my family's visits to North Dakota in the 1950s and 1960s. The "Collins girls," my mother Marian and her sisters Marjorie, Jean, and Kathleen, plus assorted female cousins, and often my great-aunts Mildred and Marian, would sit around a table in Aunt Marge's large farm kitchen, which was fragrant with cinnamon rolls and coffee. Talk would inevitably turn to the family stories of pioneering days, and tales of the eccentric "Grandma Collins" were the most intriguing. What little we knew about her at that time came from her daughter Rose, who had kept a "little black book" of Collins family history. Sadly, Rose was no longer living, and the fate of the little black book was unknown. But my mother had talked to Aunt Rose as a young woman and remembered some of the highlights.

In the 1960s, as a student of folklorist Alan Dundes at the University of California, Berkeley, I bought a tape recorder and began collecting our family's stories. Little did I realize that I would officially take on the role of "family historian." In 1991, I compiled the results of my collecting and researching in an independently published book of family history (*Dakota Dreamers*), thus fulfilling my official duties, or so I thought. As it turned out, however, I was not through with Grandma Collins.

I first learned of the Cameron diaries in July 2000, while reading an article in the magazine *Sunset*. As I skimmed over "Western Wanderings" ("Lady With a Camera," by Peter Fish), my eyes focused on two words: Terry, Montana. I recalled that Terry was the small town in the eastern part of the state where Mary Collins had lived from the early 1880s until 1909. I had often been curious about Terry.

The article tells the story of Evelyn Cameron, an aristocratic British expatriate (the locals refer to her as "Lady Cameron"), who lived in the Terry area from 1893 to 1928. She used a No. 5 Kodet camera, and later a Graflex camera—both of which used glass-plate negatives—to document the frontier life she saw around her. After her death, her work languished in a basement in Terry until 1979, when it was ferreted out by Donna Lucey, a writer who was searching for the work of frontier photographers to illustrate a Time-Life book about women pioneers. Along with a couple thousand dry-plate glass and nitrate negatives, and photo albums, Lucey discovered thirty-five volumes of diaries recording each day of Evelyn Cameron's life in Montana.

The Prairie County Museum, in Terry, has a gallery devoted to Evelyn Cameron and her photographs. One day I decided to call. Perhaps I could find a photograph of my ancestor, a feisty, eccentric, Potato Famine Irish immigrant. Although her lively reputation lives on in the Collins family lore, to our knowledge no photograph of her has survived. I guessed it was a long shot, but I hoped that Mrs. Collins might have caught the eye, and camera lens, of the photographer. At the other end of the phone was Gary Larson, a museum volunteer. He asked me about my Terry ancestor, and seemed pleasantly surprised when I said her name was Mary Collins. "Oh, yes," he replied. "Mrs. Collins." He told me that Lady Cameron had kept diaries in which she mentioned Mrs. Collins a number of times. He offered to send me a copy of a video he had made of a presentation by local actress Karen Stevenson, who had dramatized the life of Cameron in a one-woman Chautauqua performance at the museum in Terry. Her portrayal of "Lady Cameron" includes the above story about Cameron's attempt to photograph Mrs. Collins. During her performance, the detail of the borrowed false teeth got a lot of laughs.

Mr. Larson told me about Donna Lucey's book, *Photographing Montana*, which had some interesting references to my ancestor. He later kindly sent me Mary Collins' obituary from the *Terry Tribune* archive, along with the videotape of Karen Stevenson's presentation. There was also some disappointing news—he had not been able to find Mary's photograph.

Excited to discover that the two women had actually known each other, I immediately ordered a copy of *Photographing Montana*, which did contain several intriguing stories about Grandma Collins. I hoped that some day I could travel to Montana myself to visit Terry, and to see the entire collection of Cameron photographs and diaries.

When the time arrived to plan the trip, I wrote to Donna Lucey asking if she had found references to Mary Collins in the Cameron diaries in addition to the few she had included in her book. She promptly sent me a list of about twenty dates with annotations as to their content. I was thrilled, and very grateful. Even if I could not find a photograph, here was an unforeseen treasure waiting for me to unearth. My ancestor ("Mrs. Collins" in the diaries) was memorialized in this priceless document of Montana history. How would the myths passed down in my family for several generations stand up to the truths revealed about Mary Collins in Evelyn Cameron's diaries? Poking around in the family closet, I had already dislodged some skeletons—would more be uncovered?

I made the trip to Montana in June of 2003. Accompanied by my partner William, my brother Jon, and niece Jonna, who had just graduated from Berkeley High School, I visited the Montana Historical Society Archives in Helena, the repository of the Cameron Collection. The staff was very helpful, and even managed to pull one of the diaries from the "Treasures of Montana" showcase in the museum downstairs. Unfortunately, our tight schedule allowed us only one day to look at the diaries and photographs. After searching for and photocopying the pages that Donna Lucey had referred me to, I started finding even more references to Mrs. Collins, and I then realized that a thorough job would be a major task. Our visit to the photo archives, searching for Mary's photograph, was unrewarded.

As we left Helena for Terry, a day's drive away, the desk clerk at the hotel saw us off, warning: "It's really desolate out there!" At Livingston, the highway meets the Yellowstone River as it flows in a northeasterly direction to meet the Missouri River. This is the longest free-flowing river in the contiguous United States and also one of the cleanest prairie rivers. The landscape soon changes dramatically from majestic snow-capped mountains to a more open prospect. The silky surface of the Yellowstone nearly obscures the powerful current of the river as it glides past imposing sandstone bluffs to the north. The sandstone features sometimes take on whimsical and intriguing forms, such as the famous landmark Pompey's Pillar, where William Clark carved his signature in 1806 as he made his way down the river to meet Meriwether Lewis on the Missouri, following their successful expedition to the mouth of the Columbia River on the Pacific Ocean.

South of the river is the prairie: grass-covered fields, hills, ranches, and farms. Ample spring rains had left the land cloaked in green grasses, with wildflowers, sage, and an astonishing abundance of blooming yucca. The clarity of Montana's famous Big Sky cast its spell as we headed east, with a stop at Bozeman for lunch, Reed Point for gas, Forsyth for Chinese food that evening.

The next morning, after a night in Miles City, we arrived in Terry. The Prairie County Museum is a large and fascinating collection of artifacts, carefully preserved by a dedicated volunteer staff. Mary Haughian, a local resident and museum volunteer, warmly greeted us. She had previously written to me when she found out I was related to Mary Collins. She and her husband own the ranch near Terry where Mrs. Collins' grandson Lynn Ingersoll had ranched for many years. After they bought the property, until his death in 1976, Mr. Ingersoll had visited them regularly, occupying the bunkhouse and entertaining them with stories about the old days. She fondly remembers one story he told about his grandmother: she enjoyed practical jokes and loved to shock visitors. She would pull a chamber pot from under the bed and remove the lid to reveal fresh-baked cookies, which she offered to her startled guests. Her grandson, at least, had found it amusing.

Mary Haughian guided us through the collection and took us to see the Cameron gallery next door. After looking through their collection of photographs, we found none that could have been Mary Collins. However, at the County Courthouse, we did learn about the surprising number of town lots that she had bought and sold over the years, as well as about her homestead north of Terry, which we were able to locate and visit the next day.

I came home with the book *Terry Does Exist*, by B. Stith, which contains courtship letters written by John Stith, an early Terry resident, to his fiancé in Wisconsin during the first years of the town's existence. The letters describe Terry as it must have been when my great-great grandmother first arrived. (The title refers to the fact that several early histories and maps of Montana failed to mention Terry, a still-thriving town, while mentioning several towns that no longer existed.) John Stith was well acquainted with Mary Collins.

* * *

Because much of women's work on the frontier was unrecorded and is rarely mentioned in our schoolbook history lessons, Evelyn Cameron's diaries are considered a treasure of Montana history. The diaries not only provide a rare glimpse into the details of daily life in Montana of the 1890s and early twentieth century, but also document Evelyn's early struggles to learn the art of photography and turn it into a viable livelihood.

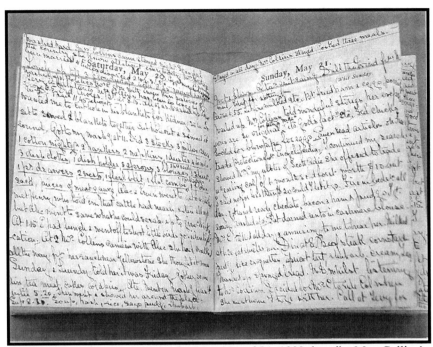

Evelyn Cameron's diary entries for May 20 and 21, 1893 describe Mrs. Collins' first visit to Eve Ranch. *Author photograph. (MC 226, Box 1, Folder 4, Montana Historical Society Research Center Archives, Helena, Montana.)*

Evelyn was well aware that her time in eastern Montana was a brief and unique moment in history and that her photographs were a record of a vanishing era. She also realized the value of recording the details of her day-to-day life. As an Englishwoman born to privilege, used to being waited on and provided for, Evelyn was proud of the ingenuity, courage, and back-breaking work that allowed her and her husband to survive in this harsh environment. In reading the diaries, one senses the relentless energy and pragmatic optimism that kept her going through times of adversity and hardship.

Back home, I began transcribing the diary pages. It was not an easy task. Evelyn often took advantage of every bit of space on the page. Reaching the bottom of a page, she would often go back up to the top and write between the lines, which often required me to use a magnifying glass to make sense of it. I did a minimal amount of editing, adding some punctuation for clarity, retaining most of the quaint Victorian spellings, but expanding many of her frequent abbreviations to avoid confusion. I tried to identify a few illegible words and phrases, and occasionally added notes in brackets.

At the top of each entry, Evelyn wrote down the most significant events of the day, underscoring them as a quick guide for future reference. Beneath the date she always recorded the day's weather, often with a remark such as "Lovely," "Glorious thunderstorm," "Dull," "Perfect day."

Once the diary entries were in an easily readable form, I was able to piece together a fascinating chapter in my great-great-grandmother's life, gleaning some insight into the indomitable pioneer of family legend, and discovering the vulnerable woman that lurked beneath. Why had she left Minnesota with her young daughter and come to this desolate place? The Cameron diaries reveal a spirited, adventurous woman, eager to escape a traumatic past. In seeking a dream of independence, Mary Collins claimed for herself a vital, if under-appreciated, role in the history of the American West, and the diaries allow at least part of her story to be told.

But another story also emerged from the diaries: two women from vastly different backgrounds struck up an unusual friendship. If Mary still harbored bitterness and anger toward the British, as the result of Ireland's genocidal sufferings during the Potato Famine, and if Evelyn felt deep-seated prejudice toward the Irish, they succeeded in laying those feelings aside. This was the American West, where newcomers were expected to embrace democratic and egalitarian values. Despite differences in class, nationality, religion, education, and age, they found a common ground. Besides being determined, resilient, and adventurous, they both had a mutual disregard for the roles to which Victorian-era women were expected to conform, as well as for conventional comforts and vanities.

Evelyn's unpretentious manner made it easy for the local people to accept her, and her diaries rarely betray a sense of social superiority. While it's impossible to know exactly what feelings existed between the two women, the diaries show that Evelyn was immensely curious about Mrs. Collins. Not only was Mary a fascinating and amusing storyteller, but she was also a valuable source of information about their neighbors—including occasional gossip and scandal. From her, Evelyn learned some of the frontier survival skills she and Ewen would need in their new life. Mary Collins must have found Evelyn to be a ready listener, an eager and intelligent younger woman to mentor, and a kind and helpful companion during their infrequent visits. The two women lived in a time and place that forced them to redefine their lives as women. They had no examples to guide the way—they had only each other's shared stories, hopes, and dreams.

Evelyn's meetings with Mrs. Collins occurred mostly in the town of Terry, and, at least in the early years, it was a rare trip to Terry that did not include a visit to Mrs. Collins. Focusing attention on these pages provides a window into Evelyn's interactions, not just with Mary, but also with the other townsfolk of Terry. The social fabric and the modest frontier economy of the town come alive through Evelyn's intriguing detail and matter-of-fact comments. Unlike many of her social class, Evelyn was not one to indulge in mawkish sentiments, or to smugly judge others.

As I read the diary pages, my curiosity led me to books about the frontier: about railroads, cowboys, and buffalo. I also read about the Irish Potato Famine, Irish women, and the Klondike gold rush. My research helped me understand the forces that were in play in the last half of the nineteenth century, and how they shaped the decisions both women made in their lives.

By this time, I had become hopelessly caught up in the story. There were some puzzling gaps in the material I had collected, and it became obvious that I would soon have to make another trip to see the Cameron diaries. The perfect opportunity presented itself in August 2005. Montana PBS had just produced a documentary film: *Evelyn Cameron: Pictures from a Worthy Life*, and planned to premier the film in Terry during a weekend of festivities. On this trip William and I managed to spend two full days at the Montana Historical Society, and came away with about a hundred photocopied diary pages relating to Evelyn's visits and conversations with

Mary Collins—and I had found answers to all my questions.

During the exciting weekend in Terry, I found time to look at more photographs in the Prairie County Museum and to visit the remains of the Cameron's first Eve Ranch. The highlight of the week, however, was meeting Donna Lucey, author of *Photographing Montana,* and Karen Stevenson, who had given me my first introduction to the diaries through her dramatic presentation.

When I met the film's producer, John Twiggs, he told me that his staff had searched for the photograph of Mrs. Collins, as they had hoped to use it in their film to illustrate the story of the missing false teeth. They had not found it.

In December 2005, as I watched a short documentary film by Kevin Costner, "America's Open Range," which accompanies the videodisc version of his excellent 2004 film *Open Range*, I was surprised when familiar photographs by Evelyn Cameron filled the screen. In this film, Costner describes Cameron's frontier experience and the importance of her photographic work. Suddenly, to my surprise, I heard a quotation from Evelyn's diary: "Went to the Collins ranch today to take pictures of Mrs. Collins. She had a great time getting herself and room ready. She couldn't find her gown and lost her false teeth . . ." For a brief moment, I hoped to see the long-lost photograph of Mrs. Collins, but instead there appeared a photograph of Evelyn's close friend Janet Williams, the young woman to whom she had bequeathed her diaries and photographs many years ago.

* * *

The friendship that evolved between Mary Collins and Evelyn Cameron, a curious one by Old World standards, was the sort of unlikely relationship that enlivens many tales of the American frontier.

From Donna Lucey's research, we know that Evelyn Cameron was born Evelyn Jephson Flower on August 26, 1868. She grew up on a large country estate south of London. Evelyn's father was an East India merchant, her mother a musician and composer. Evelyn was well educated and an avid reader. Her diaries contain occasional French and Latin phrases—one of her beloved dogs bore the name of Petrarch, a fourteen-century Italian poet. The Flower household, with fifteen servants, included older siblings from her father's prior marriage as well as six from his marriage to Evelyn's mother. There was a much older half brother, Cyril Flower, who served as a Member of Parliament and was married to Constance de Rothschild. The two moved in prominent social circles in London, and in 1892 Cyril was awarded the title Lord Battersea. Evelyn's half sister Clara was considered a great beauty.

Mary Collins, born in Ireland in 1833, came to America to escape the ravages of the Potato Famine. She never lost her thick Irish brogue, and used many quaint and amusing expressions from her native country. She knew how to write, but her awkward prose betrayed a limited education. Some may have referred to her as a "grass widow," a term meaning that a woman was either divorced or separated from her husband—it was the latter in her case. She confided to Evelyn that she had come to Montana to escape an abusive husband. Mary was one of the few women operating a business in Terry in the earliest days, keeping a large two-story boardinghouse for cowboys and railroad employees. She bought and sold a number of lots in town, and filed a claim on a homestead in her own name, which, for a woman, was unusual before the 1900s.

Mary was blessed with the Irish "gift of gab," and her lively stories no doubt contributed to her reputation as an eccentric. She also was known to utter an occasional unladylike oath, no doubt the result of her long association with rough frontier and railroad types. Her daughter Rose would remember her as tall and red-haired, enjoying an occasional beer from her supply in the cellar, and that she always wore the same disreputable hat when she went out, even on the rare times she went to church.

When they first met, Evelyn was twenty-five years old, Mary sixty. They would not become "bosom friends"—the social gulf was too great to be entirely ignored. It was more likely a strong mutual admiration that drew them together—as well as the mutual curiosity of two people from strangely different worlds. Both women were made of "stern stuff," unflinchingly accepting the harsh terms of survival on the dry eastern Montana prairie. They loved the freedom, excitement, and hard manual labor of their new lives. For them, Montana had become a refuge from their pasts, which, for different reasons, both women were happy to leave behind them.

Evelyn's family had disapproved of her choice of a mate. Ewen Cameron, a Scottish ornithologist fourteen years her senior, was often troubled by health problems, and his financial prospects were less than encouraging, despite his aristocratic background. In *Photographing Montana*, Donna Lucey describes the young couple:

> The bride was twenty-one years old, with green eyes and long, lightbrown hair swept straight back and pinned up in the style of the day. Her face was full and when she smiled she revealed a slight gap between her front teeth. Though she would hardly be called beautiful, she had a youthful, girlish charm. Ewen, fourteen years her senior, carried his slight frame with an erect bearing. His long thin face, hollow cheeks, handlebar mustache, and piercing eyes gave him a stern, even forbidding look.

On their honeymoon in 1889, Evelyn and Ewen had come to the badlands of eastern Montana primarily to hunt. Accompanied by one of the late General Custer's scouts and a cook, they hunted antelope, mule deer, mountain sheep, and grizzly bears. Excited by what they saw, they returned a year later and settled on a ranch near Miles City, where many wealthy British expatriates had come to invest in ranching.

Although Ewen came from a genteel family, he had little money, thus it was largely thanks to Evelyn's modest independent income that they were able to invest in the business of horse ranching. In 1893, they moved to a rented ranch near Terry. They called it Eve Ranch, a name they would give to all three of their Montana ranches. Aware of the Camerons' aristocratic backgrounds, local ranchers and townsfolk referred to Evelyn and her husband as "Lord and Lady Cameron"—as they do to this day. In the long run, the success they hoped for would elude them, but they proudly struggled on. Neither could face the humiliation of having to abandon their new life and return to the confining strictures of British society—and to Evelyn's disapproving family.

Soon after moving to Eve Ranch, Evelyn's brother Alec came from England to join them. The Flower family was eager, it seems, to get him off their hands, and they promised a quarterly remittance of about thirty pounds to sweeten the arrangement. In her diaries, Evelyn referred to her brother as an "idiot." (December 26, 1893) His behavior was sometimes impetuous and immature, and would create difficulties for the couple. They nearly sent him packing after a "row" on July 24, 1893: "Very hot encounter insured Ewen wanted to stand up & fight. Alec grappled. Alec tumbled over. I pulled him & slapped his bo-hind. He had torn Ewen's shirt to shreds & he was partially nude!" As it turned out, Alec would make himself useful with the animals and the garden, but he also added to Evelyn's burden of laundry, mending and cooking.

Evelyn began keeping her diaries in 1893, the first year at Eve Ranch. The 1893 volume doesn't mention her first meeting with Mary Collins, but most likely they had met at Mrs. Collins' boardinghouse in Terry. Perhaps the Camerons had spent the night during earlier visits to the area, or they may have taken their meals there, as did many ranching people when they visited Terry to stock up on supplies.

Once they had settled on their new ranch, the Camerons made it a point to seek out Mrs. Collins. On Sunday, April 30, 1893, Evelyn wrote in her diary, "I went to call on Mrs. Colins. Mrs. Jordan came to say she had gone to live on her ranch . . ." Ewen went to Terry on May 9 and reported to Evelyn that he had seen Mrs. Collins in town. It was on the afternoon of May 20 that Mary Collins set out on her four-mile walk to Eve Ranch—and the resulting encounter is where this story begins.

* * *

In writing about Evelyn Cameron and Mary Collins, I have let their story unfold as a chronological series of entries from Evelyn's diaries. Unless otherwise noted, all quotations in each chapter or

xxi

section are taken directly from the diary page cited in the heading for that chapter or section.

To help give a fuller interpretation to people and events encountered in the diaries, I have relied on research done by Donna Lucey for her book *Photographing Montana*, as well as the research of other historians whose works are cited in the text and in the bibliography.

Chapter 1

"Mrs. Collins knows all about everybody."

SATURDAY, MAY 20, 1893
Washed hard. Mrs. Collins came stayed night. Scandal.
Lovely up till 3. Clouded up little 8.45 rained hard for 5 minutes.

When Mary Collins left her homestead on the banks of the Yellowstone River to pay an unannounced visit to Evelyn and Ewen Cameron at Eve Ranch, she little suspected that it would become a much longer visit than intended. She did not own a horse, so she made the four-mile journey on foot, crossing the Northern Pacific Railroad tracks and the Terry road, following a horse and wagon track south across the narrow stretch of flat prairie. It was a glorious day. The midday sun warmed the luxuriant sage, which exuded a pleasantly tangy fragrance. The yuccas were sending up their flower spikes, and prickly pear cactuses were beginning to blossom.

She skirted a neighboring homestead, encountering Mr. Laundre, who, like herself, was one of Terry's first settlers—his name had been bestowed upon the avenue in town where Mary's boardinghouse stood facing the railroad station. Mr. Laundre thought it was Friday and wondered why Mrs. Collins would be paying a social call on a workday. Mrs. Collins was convinced that it was Sunday and, after a brief chat, continued on her way. Confusion about the day of the week was not uncommon and such a trifle did not dissuade her from her plans. She followed Ash Creek as it meandered to the southeast. Here low hills rose on either side. Finally she saw the Cameron's log house perched on the hillside. A meadowlark darted from its nest, and she made a mental note to mention it to Mr. Cameron, whose keen scientific interest in birds was already well known to residents in the area.

Evelyn Cameron had arisen at six thirty that morning. A glance in the mirror reminded her that only two days earlier a bolt of lightning had singed her hair. " I heard it burn quite plainly," she wrote. She did her chores, prepared breakfast, and washed up. Her first project of the day was a strange one: she sewed two blankets together, cut out a hole and stitched around the hole, something Ewen had requested "for kidney sore," perhaps meant to accommodate a hot or cold pack, or some kind of poultice. At eleven o'clock she began washing the large pile of laundry that had so quickly accumulated. That night in her diary she would list and underline each item she washed: "Did *3 stocks* [men's neck scarves], *3 pillow cases, 1 cotton nightgown, 2 hankers, 2 napkins, 1 duster, 4 towls, 3 dish cloths, 1 dish holder, 3 aprons, 3 blouses, 2 prs. socks, 1 shirt, 1 pr. drawers, 2 vests, 1 flannel belt, 1 flannel combi* [one-piece long underwear], *1 pr. stockings, 1 flour sack, pieces of meat gauze."* Her brother Alec went out to get some oats to feed the chickens, and at one fifteen, Ewen ate lunch and went out on a walk, "to shoot little birds for identification."

At two o'clock, Alec returned to the house in the company of a visitor—Mrs. Collins. "She had walked all the way from her ranch near Yellowstone," Evelyn noted in her diary. Visitors to Eve Ranch were few and far between. A female visitor was a rarity, and Evelyn took a break from her work to offer Mrs. Collins some food. "Got her some dinner: tea, meat, cakes, cold pies." But Evelyn did not let her guest divert her from her work—as they chatted, she continued her washing until five twenty, "then went and

Meetings With Mrs. Collins

showed her around the place." Clouds had billowed up in the afternoon, which likely induced Evelyn to insist that Mrs. Collins spend the night.

They sat down to supper at eight fifteen: "soup, hash, rice, sago [a tapioca-like starch from the pith of the sago palm] pudding, rhubarb." Dark clouds had continued to gather until, at eight forty-five, there was a brief, heavy downpour. Ewen and Mrs. Collins began a lively discussion of politics, which led to intriguing histories and scandalous gossip about Terry ranchers and townsfolk. This eccentric Irishwoman was a far cry from their wealthy and socially prominent British friends back in Miles City, but the Camerons must have realized they had found a rare local resource, an exceptionally chatty one at that. "Mrs. Collins has been so long in the country she knows all about everybody. Mrs. Jordan been married 4 times, divorced 2 or 3! C____ [a prominent local cattleman and business associate] morals disgusting," Evelyn would write in her diary that evening.

The diary does not mention where Mrs. Collins slept that night in their modest, three-room log house. Evelyn obsessively recorded the exact measurements of each room in their dwelling. The kitchen, where Evelyn often spent much of her day, measured thirteen feet, five inches by thirteen feet, one and a half inches. The Cameron's bedroom, measuring nineteen feet, nine and a half inches by twelve feet, nine and a half inches, also served as sitting room and work area where Ewen kept his volumes of ornithological studies, stuffed birds, and other tools of his trade. The only guest bed was in Alec's bedroom, which measured thirteen feet, five inches by thirteen feet, one and a half inches. Most likely Alec was obliged to spend the night on the veranda.

* * *

Mrs. Collins was considered one of the earliest settlers of Terry. The town came into being in 1881, when the Northern Pacific Railroad constructed a siding there, and the railroad began selling tickets to this stop in 1882. With the arrival of the railroad, Terry had its own brief heyday as the largest stock shipping point

Colleen Elizabeth Carter

Eve Ranch on Ash Creek, six miles from Terry, 1897. This was the first of three Cameron ranches of that name in eastern Montana. In 1893, Mary Collins walked four miles from her homestead on the Yellowstone River to pay an unannounced visit to the newcomers. *Cameron photograph, courtesy of the Prairie County Museum, Terry, Montana. (Box XVII, Neg. 339, EC19)*

in the Northwest. Mary's obituary, from the *Terry Tribune* of October 20, 1911, states that she came to Terry in 1883: "Few of the old-time stockmen in this section but well knew Mrs. Collins, her hotel being both a stopping place and home for them. Among them she had a host of friends as well as among the later arrivals in the town." It also states that, "in about 1887 she was appointed postmaster in Terry and filled this position for some time." (Her name, however, does not appear on the official list of Terry postmasters from the National Archives and Library of Congress.)

The 1885 school census lists as a student Mary's 18-year-old daughter Rose, who had accompanied her to Montana from Minnesota. Rose, however, was not on the census list for 1884, when the school opened. There is strong evidence that Mary first settled in Miles City and established a boardinghouse there before moving to Terry.

Early Terry property records show that on April 28, 1886, Mary purchased lots one and two, in block forty, for $150, from W. A. Kelly, which became the "Collins Boarding House," sometimes called the "Collins Café." Mary's business in town, and her natural loquacity, certainly put her in a position to know "all about everybody."

* * *

One man she knew well was John Stith, one of the most prominent business and civic leaders in Terry, and one of its greatest "boosters." He had arrived in 1884, following in the footsteps of his brother Frank, both of them building contractors from Wisconsin. John had left behind his fiancée, Cornelia ("Nelia") Hamilton, an "orphan girl" who had been hired as a companion to his sister, Mrs. J. A. Davies. John had two brothers, George and Frank, who were both smitten with Nelia. Each of them had unsuccessfully proposed marriage to her. The younger brother, Frank, was so upset at her refusal that he bought a ticket on the Northern Pacific Railroad to go as far as he could go, which happened to be Terry at that point.

When Frank Stith arrived, there was only a sod shack and a tent belonging to S. T. Johnson, a fur trader. Frank built a log cabin on his homestead one mile east of Terry and worked on the Joe Laundre ranch, but after his first winter in the cabin he took a room in the section house in town to be closer to his construction work.

Nelia, as it turned out, had her eye on John, the more quiet and retiring of the brothers. John decided to go west to join up with Frank. When he tried his luck with Nelia, she agreed to marry him as soon as he could build their "dream home" and establish his business in Terry. This would take much longer than the one year they had planned. John and Nelia corresponded for nearly five long years, and his courtship letters to her provide an intriguing study of Terry's early growth from a train stop with a water tank in the middle of nowhere to a lively frontier town. Selections from his letters and descriptions of the new town were published in a book

Colleen Elizabeth Carter

titled *Terry Does Exist: A History of South Eastern Montana Copied From Old Records By B. Stith*, which was prepared for the 1982 Centennial of Terry. The letters provide a human chronicle of life in Terry at the time Mary Collins would have first settled there. The quoted material that follows is taken from John's letters to Nelia.

John's first letter, of April 5, 1884, described the three-day trip from Wisconsin to Terry on the Northern Pacific Railroad, passing through Minneapolis, Fargo, and Bismark. He awoke on the morning of the third day to a desolate scene: "How lonely it looked. We traveled 32 hours without seeing a stick of timber nor even a shrub."

Early Terry settlers arrived to find the new town lying on a barren plain covered with prickly pear cactus, yucca, and sagebrush. The town was originally called Joubert's Landing, after a settler who sold fuel wood to passing steamboats on the Yellowstone River. The name was later changed to Terry Station, after General Alfred H. Terry, commander in the six-year war against the Sioux—during which General Custer had met his doom in July of 1876.

The discouraging landscape, as well as his painful separation from Nelia, caused him to fret over his decision to join his brother in Terry. When the train arrived in the tiny town, he found Frank at work building the new Zahl Hotel. "I looked at him and at myself and at the surrounding country and wondered if I was myself or a desperado. I said to Frank, 'Hurry up and get ready so we can take the next train back.'"

Frank managed to calm his brother, and took him to the hotel where he had a room and a bed "pile" for which he had paid $25. "Bord here is $4.50 per week and they furnish you a room but you haf to furnish your own bed. Franks bed consists of 3 Blankets one quilt and a buffalo skin." On April 14, John wrote: "I am not in love with the country and worst of all I don't think you would be but I do not want to go away unless Frank will go with me for I think we can do better together."

John had another serious concern: there were forty men to every woman. Newly arrived women, whether married or not, were the object of male "attentions," and some quickly discovered that they could have their pick of eligible men. It was not unusual for a young woman to leave her husband for another man, a practice that John found reprehensible. He did not want to risk exposing his fiancé to this "rush."

On September 21, 1884, John wrote more encouragingly about the town: "Terry seems like quite a different place. Their has been three nice familys came here . . . Their is considerable of building going to be done this fall." On October 28, he reported: "Last spring there was only 3 girls in Terry. Now there are twelve." His letters became more upbeat—he told of lively cowboy dances, new "schoolmarms," and the Terry Opera Troupe, a theatrical group in which he was an enthusiastic participant.

Within several miles of Terry there grew an abundance of wild plums, grapes, choke cherries, and a variety of berries, which residents sought when they grew tired of the dried apples shipped from back East. Eventually residents would make use of the ample supply of underground water to transplant some of the wild species to their lots in town. John reported that the soil was rich enough to grow vegetables of unimaginable size: "A farmer brought in a load of potatoes yesterday that will average over 4 lbs. One potato would make a mess for quite a family. Also a Rheutibago weighing 17 1/2 lbs. . . ."

When an itinerant minister from Iowa held a multi-denominational church service in Terry on January 5, 1885, John wrote, "It looked strange to see the cowboys go to church with their six shooters on. The discourse lasted to long for some of the congregation. They had to go out to the saloon too or three times during church to get a drink."

In 1884, John bought lot eighteen in block forty on which he intended to build Nelia's "dream home," but financial difficulties and a series of natural disasters threatened to destroy his chances for success. The summer of 1886 brought drought and terrible grass fires, soon followed by the disastrous winter of 1886-87, which threatened to crush all his hopes. It was the worst on record, in some areas killing as much as ninety percent of cattle and sheep.

The brutal cold that winter brought to a halt a brief period of over-expansion in the cattle industry. Texas cattlemen had been holding on to their stock, trying to wait out a slump in prices. They moved huge numbers of cattle into Montana to escape drought in the southern plains. But the summer had been dry in Montana too. The huge herds overgrazed the land, and when the blizzard struck, the weakened cattle were trapped and frozen in large numbers. In his Stith Hardware customer accounts book John wrote: "Lots of ranches and some businessmen have gone broke." The next summer his hopes were raised when he got the contract to build Terry's first schoolhouse (classes had previously been held in the wool storage warehouse).

Many cattle ranchers and other settlers had given up after the terrible winter and were leaving southeastern Montana. Among them was John's brother Frank. He relinquished his homestead and moved his log house to John's lot in town. Frank then left for Washington in November 1887, and soon moved on to Oregon. Letters arrived from Frank extolling the beauty of the country, urging John to come west with Nelia.

January 1888 brought another siege of cold, snow, and ice. It swept down from Canada on the eleventh, and moved into Dakota Territory by the next morning, building strength as it progressed across the plains. By the afternoon of the twelfth it had trapped and killed hundreds of settlers on the plains, including schoolchildren in their one-room schoolhouses, lured out by a warming trend earlier in the day. Although the storm did not cause much death and destruction in eastern Montana, it did create problems for John Stith in the early spring, postponing a much-needed contracting job on the north side of the Yellowstone River. But later that year John got the contract to build the Jordan Hotel in Terry, and now he could finally send for Nelia to join him. By the time the hotel was nearly completed, however, John had succumbed to Frank's entreaties. He quickly sold his house, arranged to sell his business, and was ready to go west with Nelia as soon as she arrived.

To his surprise, Nelia refused to leave the place where he had made so many friends and established a business. Five years of John's letters had done their work only too well, and Nelia had grown to know and love the town of Terry and its residents. They

Meetings With Mrs. Collins

Stith Hardware, Terry, Montana, built in 1884. John Stith, who settled in Terry that year, soon became one of the town's leading citizens. *Cameron photograph, courtesy of the Prairie County Museum, Terry, Montana.(Box XIX, Neg. 3, EC39)*

were married in Miles City on September 22, 1888. The couple stayed in the new Jordan Hotel until John could buy their house back.

The years that followed brought success to the Stiths and established John as a community leader: Justice of the Peace, School Clerk, Custer County Commissioner. He took on responsibility for the sheep ranchers' wool when it was brought to Terry for shipment to eastern markets. His new store prospered as his contracting business grew. Nelia made her own contribution to the community. She had received nurse's training back in Wisconsin and was much in demand for her services. The people of Terry, living far from a doctor, came to borrow emergency remedies from her well-stocked medicine cabinet.

This, then, was the town of Terry, where Mary Collins settled sometime between 1883 and 1885. She would have many dealings with the Stiths. In later years, she would sell John Stith one of her lots in town, and he would help her with an important legal matter.

Nelia Stith was the postmistress in Terry when Evelyn and Ewen Cameron first arrived, and she became one of Evelyn's earliest friends. On February 26, 1893, shortly after moving to Eve Ranch, Evelyn reported that "Mrs. Stith's 'acouchment' [a French euphemism for childbirth] took place 24th." Two days later, she paid a visit, finding the new mother in bed: "The baby was shown to me such a poor looking little thing. I said nice things about it." On March 21, Mrs. Stith gave Evelyn "a young tom cat which I took home in a gunny sack. This [is] the prettiest kitten I have ever seen & I have named it 'Cinders.'"

Chapter 2

"Mrs. C. talked all day, amusing to me to hear her."

SUNDAY, MAY 21, 1893
Stayed in all day. Mrs. Collins stayed. Cooked 3 meals.
Wet & blowy. Afternoon quit raining. Dull . . . [illegible] wind from North.

It was a cold morning at Eve Ranch, and the rain forced Mrs. Collins to extend her visit. Except for trips to the barn to milk the cows and feed the chickens, the Camerons and their guest stayed inside all day. Evelyn prepared a breakfast of "fried ham & eggs, porridge." In her diary, she would write, "Mrs. Collins told wonderful stories, her expressions are so original: 'for pity's sake,' 'it's god's fact,' etc." After breakfast, Ewen read aloud "articles on free trade protection from Encyclopedia."

Evelyn, however, could not afford to sit idle. While listening to Mrs. Collins and Ewen, she embarked on a futile search for something called a "blowpipe for eggs," probably used to preserve the bird eggs collected on Ewen's walk the previous day. As Donna Lucey explains:

It is evident from Evelyn's diaries that Ewen spent most of his days absorbed in observing and writing about Montana wildlife, especially the birds. Evelyn was an invaluable partner in his work: she accompanied him on many an "ornithological ramble"; she helped him amass an extensive collection of eggshells by carefully blowing out their contents . . .

That morning Evelyn showed Mary her cherished skirt, which she called an "ulster of Scott Adie." Mrs. Collins, very taken with it, "offered to trade a yearling calf of 6 months for it worth $10, but I said not for less than $20 could I let it go."

Evelyn kept the fire going all day, using coal, which homesteaders collected in wagons from the generous outcroppings to be found in the badlands north of the Yellowstone River. Lunch consisted of "chocolate, bacon & ham & puddings." Mrs. Collins continued to talk while Evelyn washed up and "darned rents in cashmere blouse. Mrs. C. talked all day, amusing to me to hear her." In addition to gossip, frontier women shared useful household tips. At a later date Mrs. Collins would advise Evelyn to wash her floor with whey.

As the rain eased up in the afternoon, Evelyn went out to milk the cows and feed corn to the chickens. At eight o'clock they sat down to dinner: "Beefsteak, cornstarch pudding, rice croquettes, apricot tart, rhubarb, cream, tea." Blessed with the Irish "gift of gab," Mrs. Collins continued talking into the evening as Evelyn washed up and prepared the "sponge" for a batch of bread. (Donna Lucey explains that Evelyn "kept on hand a batch of starter dough—yeast, which she grew on cooked potatoes, mixed with flour and water—a concoction she referred to as her 'sponge.'" Evelyn reported taking it to bed with her in winter to keep it from freezing.)

Evelyn even managed to write in her diary "whilst listening to Mrs. Collins." Prior to turning in for the night they discussed their plans for the next day. Evelyn offered to accompany Mrs. Collins home on horseback, Mrs. Collins riding the gentle horse named Col. They would "call at Terry for mail" before going to Mrs. Collins' homestead.

Meetings With Mrs. Collins

It had been a long, exhausting day, even though the poor weather had kept Evelyn from much of her strenuous outdoor labor. Sunday's diary entry ended: "Tired for nothing."

* * *

"Total of eggs so far this yr. 599."
—Evelyn Cameron diary, July 1893

13

Chapter 3

"Curious little building, narrow & high."

MONDAY, MAY 22, 1893
<u>Rode with Mrs. Collins down to Terry & to her house. Dinner there. Back 6.45.</u>
Lovely morn. Became cloudy, shower bout 4.

After morning chores and breakfast, Evelyn saddled the horses, "Andy for me, Col for Mrs. Collins." While going to the garden to pick some rhubarb for Mrs. Collins, Evelyn fell and strained her left knee "painfully." There was a long delay while Ewen took the horse Andy up to their neighbor's ranch "to have hoofs pared," but Henry Tusler, who helped them with such work, had left for Miles City.

They finally got off at about twelve twenty, Evelyn wearing her dark blue riding habit. "Ewen came with us to see a Meadow Lark's nest Mrs. Collins knew of, but tho' they searched patiently didn't find it. We went on alone." It's likely that Mary was unaccustomed to horseback riding, since Evelyn noted that they "walked all the way." During their leisurely ride, Evelyn continued to learn about Terry's locals. They discussed a man named Billy Whipple, a local carpenter and violinist: "Mrs. Collins has known a very long time & has a very high opinion of him."

They stopped at the post office on Logan Avenue, in the home of Nelia Stith, and picked up their mail. Evelyn had wanted to buy a lemon for her brother Alec, who suffered from a "bilious attack this morn." They went to "Mrs. C's Jordan, who did not have any." Mary's oft-divorced friend, Mrs. W. F. Jordan was another of Terry's earliest settlers. She ran the Jordan Hotel in Terry, and since she had received nurse's training in Chicago, the townsfolk depended on her—as they did on Mrs. Stith—for medical advice and supplies in times of illness. Her husband ran a store that sold "General Merchandise, Groceries, Dry Goods, Clothing, Etc."

Mary and Evelyn rode east a mile from town, to the Collins "ranch," a quarter section homestead, 160 acres, the northeast corner of which touched the banks of the Yellowstone River. Mary Collins had "proved up" on her claim and acquired the deed to her homestead just the month before. It's likely that she had hired—or bartered for—help to erect the small house that was needed to fulfill one of the homesteading requirements. Evelyn noted that it was a "curious little building, narrow & high." Perhaps Mary had upstairs sleeping quarters like the home she had left in Minnesota. If so, it would not have been the typical single-story homestead "shack," most no larger than the required minimum ten by twelve feet. These simple dwellings, made of logs, lumber, or even tarpaper, had a "dollhouse" quality that must indeed have seemed "curious." An undecipherable sentence in the diary entry mentions something about water—there is a huge pond at the eastern edge of the property, and after the storm the low-lying areas may have been very wet.

Family legend claims that Mary operated a ferry that crossed the Yellowstone River to the north side. There were a number of such ferries run by entrepreneurial homesteaders, and women owned a few of them. In fact, the first ferry mentioned in Terry records belonged to Mrs. Joe Laundre, who sold it to Frank Stith in 1886. In 1895, on their annual winter hunting trip, the Camerons would cross to the north side of the Yellowstone on a ferry outside

Meetings With Mrs. Collins

Mary Collins was granted the certificate for this 160-acre homestead on April 8, 1893. The northeast corner of the property touches the Yellowstone River, where, according to family legend, Mary operated a ferry. The badlands can be seen in the background. *Collection of author.*

Miles City run by a Mrs. Curry and a Miss Hamilton. One of Mary's stories that got passed down in family lore told of the time she ferried a mysterious stranger across the river. The man explained that he could not pay her, but if she would come back to the same spot in a few nights there would be some money waiting for her. When she returned, she found ten dollars, a considerable sum considering that cowboys earned monthly wages of about thirty dollars. Something about the man, and the peculiar circumstances, led Mary to suspect that he must have been a "highwayman."

Mrs. Collins prepared a lunch for her guest of "bacon, potatoes, canned peaches, tea, bread," a less elegant spread than Evelyn was accustomed to, but the sort of modest rations Mary might have kept on hand, since she divided her time between the homestead and her boardinghouse in town. The canned peaches, however, would have been considered a treat. Now that she had Evelyn to herself, Mary embarked on a more intimate conversation: "Mrs. C. told me she left her husband in 1870. He had such a violent temper [she was] afraid of her life. He has married again since, bigamy."

They chatted until late in the afternoon. Evelyn arrived home at six forty-five. "Picked flowers on way."

* * *

Mary's husband, Patrick Collins, served in the Union Army during the Civil War in Minnesota's Third Regiment, Company K. There is a story passed down in our family that he was "wounded in the head at the Battle of Murfreesboro." In his old age Patrick lived for a period of time with his son James Collins in Page, North Dakota. His grandson, William Collins—my grandpa—claimed that you could still see the wound. His military records, however, tell a different story. It is true that his regiment fought at the Battle of Murfreesboro, which took place in 1862, but Patrick didn't enlist in the army until two years later, on February 2, 1864—when the war was nearly over. In fact, new recruits were told that Union Forces were close to winning the war and that their tour of duty would be a short one.

Although he seems not to have seen active fighting, it is clear that he suffered. Patrick spent the final eighteen months of the war near Pine Bluff, Arkansas, much of the time ill with malaria. The camp surgeon's report states that, at first, conditions in the camp were so unhealthy that "eight-tenths were stricken down of malarial fever, and eighty-nine died . . . We suffered here very much for the want of medical supplies . . . I am free to say I would much rather have been in a hard fought battle every week during the summer (in a healthy locality) than to spend such a summer in that deadly locality." When some of the soldiers went home in August on veteran furlough, " . . . many of the poor fellows were so lean and pale that their own mothers could scarcely have recognized them."

Meetings With Mrs. Collins

The war ended in April 1865, and it's likely that Patrick was sent home then, although his official date of discharge was September 16, 1865, at Fort Snelling, Minnesota. His oldest daughter, Mary Madore ("Mamie" or "Maude"), was nine years old, Sarah E. was five, and James F., my great-grandfather, was two. Patrick and Mary wasted no time in enlarging their family, and a daughter, Rose, was born on January 17, 1866.

Then life for the Collins family took a turn for the worse. Documents in Patrick's military and pension records reveal that he left his family in 1870, moved to Glenco, Minnesota, and remarried—without the benefit of a divorce from Mary. He was later arrested on a charge of bigamy. As Mary would state in an affidavit in 1909, she saw him only two or three times after he deserted her, and that as far as she knew "he led a wandering life." It may have been these later visits that gave rise to his "violent temper," prompting her to seek refuge in Montana, where she hoped to avoid her abusive husband and achieve economic independence.

Patrick, unfortunately, fulfilled the stereotype of the abusive, probably drunken, possibly mentally unbalanced, Irish husband, all too common both in Ireland and in America. The Catholic Church would not sanction their divorce, and Mary would sometimes refer to herself as a widow, and Patrick would claim that he was a widower, probably to avoid the stigma of divorce or separation.

Although Patrick provided no support for his family after 1870, Mary retained a small property in the village of High Forest, near Rochester, Minnesota. It consisted of "one lot 66 feet wide and 132 feet long . . . with house thereon—House 16 feet by 18 feet two story high . . . House and lot worth $ 100 [in 1909]." This may or may not have been part of the 40-acre parcel originally purchased by Patrick Collins in 1861 for $1.25 an acre from the government, the deed granted by President Abraham Lincoln.

Mary and her children do not appear in the Minnesota federal census for 1870.

* * *

I visited Terry with the hope of finding Mary's homestead site, and I also wanted to see if the building where she ran her boardinghouse had survived (it had not—the old Northern Pacific train depot now stands in its place). A courthouse record search disclosed the surprising extent of her property. In addition to the homestead, she had owned eight lots in Terry. The history of the purchases and sales sheds light on Mary's life and aspirations.

The Homestead Act of 1862 enabled "any person who is the head of a family, or who has arrived at the age of twenty-one years" and was or intended to become a U.S. Citizen, to file for a quarter section of free land. The act allowed single, divorced, widowed, and other women who were heads of households to file claims in their own names. Older and younger single women, widows with and without children, divorced and deserted women, and even some married women, who were considered the heads of their households because their husbands were ill or incapacitated, became homesteaders. The act required homesteaders to pay a fourteen dollar filing fee and granted them five years to improve, or "prove up," their land. During these five years, the applicant could not change residency or abandon his or her legal claim for more than six consecutive months at any given time.

Historians have largely ignored the fact that thousands of women homesteaded on the prairies. Mary was part of a significant movement of women from many walks of life, of varying ages, and with differing goals and strategies, who sought freedom and independence on the prairie. But certain aspects of Mary's experience set her apart from the majority of women homesteaders. First, she was one of a tiny minority of women over the age of fifty who applied for land. Second, at the time she filed, in the late 1880s, she was one of a very few women who had taken advantage of the Homestead Act in Montana—the majority of women filed after 1900. Third, the most common pattern for women was to file on land adjacent to friends or family members, thus assuring an instant "mutual aid society." Mary fit more into the category of "lone adventurer," but by the time she filed her claim she had been in the Terry area long enough to have made many close friends. Homesteaders found that neighbors were quick to help each other in obtaining the necessities of life; there was frequent informal visiting, and considerable cooperation and bartering.

The pattern in which Mary bought and sold property reveals another way in which she did not fit the norm—she appears to have been speculating in real estate. Since she filed on her homestead claim in 1888, a year after the severe winter that caused so many to leave, it's possible she was able to file a claim on the land of a homesteader who had given up and sold out.

In common with many women who homesteaded, Mary had an alternate means of making a living: she operated a boardinghouse, and also set up cooking tents at the Fallon cattle roundup. After acquiring the homestead, Mary divided her time between the boardinghouse in town and the homestead, where she put in the legally required time to fulfill the obligations of her claim. It was common for women, as well as men, to barter for, or hire out, some of the building and tilling jobs on the homestead. But there were still many routine domestic chores which were usually considered to be traditional women's work: cooking, baking, churning butter, washing, mending, gardening and tending poultry and cows. Mary did many of these jobs on her homestead, in addition to the exhausting work of running her boardinghouse in Terry: washing and mending bed linens, making beds, preparing and serving meals, baking, and constant cleaning. As reward for her hard work, the boardinghouse established Mary as a successful entrepreneur, giving her considerable status in the community.

Chapter 4

"Great agony displayed was heartrending."

THURSDAY, SEPTEMBER 28, 1893
Ewen & I rode to Fallon. Saw cattle loaded on cars. Mr. Coggshall, Lisk, etc.
Beautiful morn. Afternoon cloudy, warm. S.W. breeze.

After a breakfast of oatcakes, Ewen and Evelyn prepared for a much-anticipated excursion—they would spend the afternoon at the stockyards in the town of Fallon, nine miles east of Terry. The town was named after Benjamin O'Fallon, an Indian agent, and a nephew of William Clark. During the 1890s, Fallon became a major stock-shipping center.

The Camerons looked forward to watching the ranchers and cowboys loading cattle and horses onto railroad cars for shipment to markets back east. Mrs. Collins would be there, operating her profitable cook tents. On June 24, she had told Evelyn that it would take her a month to "get fixed [for] wood Etc." before she could leave for the "O'Fallon" roundup.

Colleen Elizabeth Carter

* * *

By 1893, the legendary era of the open range and long cattle drives had passed its peak. In eastern Montana, the cattle drives had begun a decade earlier, when the Northern Pacific Railroad opened the territory to a vast market potential in the eastern states. When the rangelands in Texas became overgrazed and affected by drought, and Kansas and Missouri established quarantines against Texas cattle—which had spread "Texas Fever" to domestic cattle in those states—the cattle were driven north. They followed the famous Texas Trail, passing through seven states. The longhorns, descended from wild cattle introduced by Spaniards 300 years before, fattened up on the nutritious bunch grass of the northern prairies, then were rounded up and loaded onto freight cars.

The discovery of these public domain lands of free grass and water brought on a boom in ranching that attracted investors—wealthy Easterners, English, and Scots—and the ranch lands became overstocked. Soon, a better breed of cattle, the descendents of livestock originally taken by pioneers into Oregon and Washington thirty years earlier, were being driven east across the Rockies and would eventually replace the longhorns in the northern ranges. Ranchers then needed to protect their investments: barbed wire fences went up, wells were sunk, windmills erected, barns built, fields irrigated and planted.

The largest and most famous of the cattle ranches in the Fallon area was the XIT. Its headquarters was in the Texas panhandle, where this mega-ranch spread out over 3,050,000 acres. The name XIT, "Ten In Texas," referred to the ten counties in Texas covered by this outfit, which was controlled by Chicago capitalists. XIT also leased 15,000 square miles of Montana rangeland.

"Teddy Blue" Abbott, a Texas cowboy whose memoirs, *We Pointed Them North,* capture the essence of the open range era, states that the long trail drives on the Texas Trail ended in 1895, after the XIT Ranch brought its three last herds to Montana.

Other large operations were the Keeline of Wyoming, also known as "Hog's Eye," due to its distinctive eye-shaped brand, the LX, also of Wyoming, and the Standard Cattle Company of Boston. The Texas cowboys who came north with the herds liked what they saw, and many stayed on, earning good pay on ranches run by wealthy cattlemen.

There were also local ranches, such the "13 Ranch" with its notoriously wild cowboys. One of them, "Tobacco Jack," ran "quite a-muck" in Miles City in 1885. A news report called him "the champion wiper-out of the Northwest." While trying to kill a Mr. Sullivan in a bar with his "gigantic pistol" he only succeeded in wounding a bystander. Before taking Jack into custody, the sheriff was obliged to chase the man through town. "The open saloon doors all invited a shot from his gun, and the wonder is that the 'champion wiper-out' hadn't a dozen new notches to cut on his revolver stocks to represent dead he'd planted."

John Stith, who was acquainted with Tobacco Jack, sent the news clipping to his fiancé along with the comment: "Tobacco Jack (or his rite name Frank Allen) is one of our Terry Cow Boys and is working on the 13 Ranch nere here. He takes the lead at all our partys. He is always Jolly and tryes to make evry one else so. Of corce he is wild Cow Boy stile and too much given to drink for reason he was telling me the other night that he had been crossed in love."

John's letter of the previous month had described the wild aftermath of a cowboy dance in the hotel where he was boarding. "I did not go to the dance myself, John wrote, "but those that did go say the dance went off nicely and a good time was had by all, but after the dance broke up this morning the cow boys began to drink and shoot. They broke windows, doors, lamps, and smashed up things in great shape around town. About one o'clock this afternoon, a cowboy went in the Livery Stable to get his horse. He had a six shooter in each hand, and wanted to fight. The livery man refused to fight so the cowboy took him over town and made him kneel on every door step and ask their forgiveness." It was not long before the citizens of Terry built a jail and elected two constables, putting an end to such lawlessness.

Barbed wire had begun partitioning off the once-open range. Sheep ranchers and, later, farmers gradually replaced the cattle ranchers, a process that would be completed in the early 1900s—especially after the hard winter of 1903 - 1904 dealt a final death-

Colleen Elizabeth Carter

The XIT cowboys were among those who frequented Mary Collins' cook tents in Fallon during the fall roundup. The XIT Ranch, headquartered in the Texas panhandle, where it covered more than three million acres, also leased 15,000 square miles of Montana rangeland near Fallon.
Cameron photograph, courtesy of the Prairie County Museum, Terry, Montana.
(Box VIII, Neg. 20, EC17)

blow to the cattle industry in southeastern Montana

* * *

On this beautiful September day, the Camerons would get a glimpse of the cowboy's way of life. They had heard much about these courageous, exuberant young men, who were already Western legends and dime-novel heroes. The long cattle drives may have been a thing of the past, but the Fallon roundup still evoked that romantic era.

Before leaving home, Evelyn gathered forty to fifty pounds of cabbages and sweet corn and put them in flour sacks to deliver to Mrs. Collins. The Camerons left their ranch at about eleven fifteen.

Meetings With Mrs. Collins

"Down creek round our new fence we made our way to the traveled road. Got to a full running spring. Past a hogs eye wagon & another also."

Arriving at Fallon, they immediately delivered the sacks of vegetables to Mrs. Collins in her cook tents near the railroad tracks. The Camerons took their dinner there, "Beef stew, potatoes, custard pie," which Evelyn would rate "very good." Mrs. Collins gave Evelyn "her debts and receipts," which shows that there was an ongoing business arrangement between them.

The Camerons rode their "osses" [horses] on to the stock pens and tied them up. Sitting up on the "top runs" they could observe the Keeline cattle, as they were loaded into a railroad car. It was rough work. One cow broke its horn: "Great agony displayed was heartrending." They watched a two-year-old being roped: "It broke puncher's rope." A boy jumped down and grabbed the end of the rope off the cow and "jumped back out before [it] could hurt him." They watched the cattle being driven into corrals: "Drive bunch of osses in front to make cattle go into pens." Then they returned to the cattle cars and watched the loading until 5:25.

Before leaving town, Evelyn and Ewen stopped to see Mrs. Collins again. "She wanted us to take supper." They apparently declined, since after reaching home they had "Supper rewarmed." Before retiring at eleven o'clock, Evelyn "made bulberry jelly for next morning. Put in pail."

* * *

Today, more than a hundred years later, there is little to show of the town that was once Fallon. In 1894, the town consisted of a section house, a general store, and a log house that did double duty as a post office. The big cattle investors did little to contribute to building up the town. On the other hand, Terry became a major wool-shipping point. Many of the surrounding ranches were owned by sheep ranchers, who lived on their land and paid taxes. Today it is the county seat—blessedly free of suburban sprawl and fast-food joints—whose proud citizens cherish its historic buildings and tradition of community spirit.

Chapter 5

"I pity poor old Mrs. Collins in her tents in this sort of weather."

SATURDAY, SEPTEMBER 30, 1893
Shucked corn, swept store house. Sewed afternoon. All sat in kitchen.
Very wet all day. Later cold North wind.

Two days after the Cameron's visit to Fallon, a cold wet storm blew in from the north. Evelyn finished her usual morning chores and then worked in the storehouse until twelve thirty. "Took husks off of late corn & spread them (cobs) on floor to dry. Gave horses husks in manger. They liked them very much." She prepared lunch, "a meager one," after which she sat by the kitchen stove and sewed, mended, and "plaited seed squaw corn together."

She worked industriously as the men relaxed and read. "Ewen read ghost story to me out of 'Black & White,' [a] stupid one. [*Black & White* was among the reading materials that Ewen's mother sent from Scotland.] Alec sat, read aloud curious notes to me." After preparing a hearty meal of "veal pie, 3 teal duck, potatoes, tomatoes, thick sauce, sago pudding, choke cherry pie," she washed up and "damped clothes" for ironing the next day.

It was taken for granted that Evelyn's chores were "women's work." The men could justify taking the day off during rainy weather, but for the woman of the house it was just another day of work. Prior to her marriage, Evelyn had led a pampered life and was unlikely to have performed household chores. The fact that, during her early years in Montana, she itemized in her diary each job completed, every piece of clothing laundered, and every meal prepared, indicates pride in her self-sufficiency and hard manual labor. In her diary that night, however, she remarked wearily, "Ewen says I stoop so fearfully. My back becomes tired so often and aches."

But Evelyn was not one to focus much sympathy on herself, and her thoughts wandered back to Fallon, where Mary Collins had endured another exhausting day: "It poured hard all day, with 2 or 3 intervals of rest," she wrote. "I pity poor old Mrs. Collins in her tents in this sort of weather."

Evelyn was uniquely qualified to sympathize with Mrs. Collins. Each fall, the Camerons went on an extended hunting trip, sometimes lasting a month or more, into the badlands north of the Yellowstone River, and Evelyn would soon need to begin preparations. While preparing for the following year's hunt, Evelyn would complain, "V[ery] tired on legs. I can appreciate the feelings of a cab horse 'When down can't get up.'" (October 13, 1894)

On these trips—as at Eve Ranch—Evelyn found herself bearing the brunt of the work. Not only did she perform the cooking and camp duties, but she also tended the horses and did the cleaning and skinning of the game. The excursions were often made under adverse, even dangerous, conditions.

On this November trip they took a young hired hand named Lester Braley. On the evening of November 12, the Camerons returned to camp to find that their tent had caught fire and that most of their supplies were wet from Braley's attempts to put it out. That night Evelyn noted: "Sup outside. Coyottes howled very much quite close . . . Fire must have started on the dry grass around the Sibley stove [a cast iron wood-burning stove invented during the Civil War and used extensively throughout the West. It was an inverted cone with a stovepipe that went up through a hole in the center of the tent. Many a tent was set on fire by them.] Wrote diary by big fire." (Even today, the pages she filled on that trip are coated with a thin film of grit.) They slept in what remained of their tent, and the next morning they awoke to a "Fearfully strong & cold West wind. Rose 7:20. O' so wretchedly uncomfortable." Nearby was an empty ranch shack, which they moved into. Despite odors of the dead steer and the large quantity of manure Braley had labored to remove, Evelyn cheerfully proclaimed, "Our shack seems so luxurious after last night & this morn."

* * *

Evelyn used the blank pages in the back of her diaries to track the productivity of her garden and egg-laying hens, and also to record her written correspondence for the year. She sometimes copied the text of letters she wrote, but more often simply noted the contents. There she recorded a letter from Mrs. Collins, dated November 15 and received November 24, 1893: "Wishes us to take care of her cow & calf this winter." Evelyn responded to her letter on November 26, "stating willingness to pasture her cow & calf through the winter." On December 18, Mary sent yet another letter, "about the cow's good qualities. She would like 100 pounds of potatoes." By then, Mary had gotten her cow and calf up to Eve Ranch before winter weather set in. Her solicitous comments about the cow reflect the honored position a milk cow enjoyed in a frontier household—much like that of a valued family member.

On New Year's Day, 1894, Evelyn bagged up the potatoes, along with fifty-two pounds of turnips. By evening, however, she noticed: "Wind [is] blowing strongly from N. am afraid I shall not be able to make the trip tomorrow, the potatoes would freeze." On January 2, she recorded another letter to Mrs. Collins: "Frustrated intention of carrying potatoes to her (by weather)."

Colleen Elizabeth Carter

In early 1894, Evelyn recorded further transactions with Mrs. Collins. On March 15: "When at P.O. saw Mrs. Collins house opened up so I rode over & found Mrs. C. there she was getting her house ready. We chatted [she] wants lbs. 200 of my potatoes will give 2¢ all = $2 a hundred."

Ewen delivered 300 pounds of "taters" to Mrs. Collins on March 23. When Evelyn was in Terry the next day she "went to Mrs. Collins got $1 from her on potatoe acct. . . ." She collected the balance of five dollars on April 1.

* * *

"Do the work that's nearest,
Though it's dull at whiles,
Helping when you meet them,
Lame dogs over stiles."

"Work on, Hope on,
Self help is noble schooling,
You do your best & leave the rest
To God Almighty's ruling."
—Written inside the front cover of Evelyn's 1901 diary.

Chapter 6

"She is such a rum 'un."

TUESDAY, MAY 8, 1894
<u>Ewen & I rode to Terry. Dinner with Collins. Drove up calf & cow.</u>
Lovely. Wind S. strong lulled. 10.30 Very warm [gusts?] to N.

Evelyn arose at five thirty. After morning chores and breakfast she realized, "my tooth feels quite well no need to see Dr. Adams again." The day before, she and her neighbor, Mrs. Drew, had visited an itinerant dentist in Terry: "Cost me $7 to have 3 teeth stop [filled]. Mrs. Drew $10 job. Hurt me awfully & not sure it would not bleed & have to be pulled or nerve killed."

Ewen drove their cows up "to the bull" in their neighbor's pasture. During his absence, Mrs. Drew's lively little boy Jack showed up. "He fidgetted about & wanted us to put a rope round his waist & drag him to Terry."

When Ewen returned, the Camerons left for Terry on horseback and, after collecting their mail, went to see Mrs. Collins. "She kept me very much amused with her gossip and incessant jabbed [jabbered] whilst she prepared dinner of ham, fried eggs, boiled potatoes, cake. Very good."

Later in the afternoon, the Camerons "mounted & had a great time getting Mrs. C's cow & calf away from Terry at last after a lot of charging drove them off from shacks & barns. Got home by 5 put them in big pasture."

* * *

WEDNESDAY, MAY 9, 1894
<u>Ewen & I drove Collins cow to Terry din with Mrs. C. Home 3.30</u>
Dreadfully windy from the N. Cold too. Evening cleared.

Evelyn arose at five fifteen. She milked the cows, then served a substantial breakfast: "Scrambled eggs, fried bacon, curry, rice, coffee, tea."

Her diary entry explains the prior day's exertions with Mrs. Collins' cow and calf: "At about X.20 [10:20] I think, we rode into the big [pasture] & brought Collins cow & calf up to the corral, Mr. Adams [a friend of Alec's who had come to live with them as a boarder] led the cow with halter & rope up to gate. Ewen led her on Joe & I drove her behind to the outside of Coyle's new fence then drove her. We left her with some cows outside Terry." In this way they separated the cow from its calf, which they most likely had purchased from Mrs. Collins. The Camerons yielded to Mrs. Collins' insistence that they come in for a "cup of tea," but once inside, "she gave us coffee, ham, eggs, potatoes, etc. Talked as usual in her comic strain incessantly."

That evening Evelyn wrote, "I spent all the afternoon in trying to halter break the Collins calf but even with Mr. Adam's help insuccessful, so terribly obstinate got on the fight & charged me & the fence. Tied it up." After supper Evelyn put the calf out in the pasture. Although Evelyn had an unusual affinity for animals, and was known for her gentleness and patience in breaking stubborn and unruly horses, the new calf, separated from its mother, proved extremely uncooperative.

Meetings With Mrs. Collins

* * *

THURSDAY, MAY 10, 1894
<u>Mrs. Collins walked up. Her cow & calf we drove down [in the] afternoon.</u>
Glorious day. So bright & nice North breeze.

Evelyn served a breakfast of "herrings, bacon & eggs," and then went about her morning chores. Ewen went outside to work, but soon came back into the house to let Evelyn know that he had spotted Mrs. Collins approaching the ranch house on foot. Evelyn wrote: "I went out & found her sitting by the fence of [the] new pasture with her felt shoes & socks off picking cactus thorn out of her feet! She is such a rum 'un' [a British expression meaning "eccentric" or "peculiar."]." Lewis and Clark would not have recommended wearing "felt shoes" in eastern Montana. The thorns Mary was picking out of her feet were from the low-growing Prickly Pear Cactus, *Opuntia polyacantha,* of which Meriwether Lewis wrote in his journal, "[it is] one of the beauties as well as the greatest pest of the plains." Mary was likely muttering a few Irish curses as she extracted the thorns from her feet.

She had come out in search of her cow, correctly guessing that it had wandered back to Eve Ranch, lonely for its calf. Evelyn quickly put some food on the stove: "veal, cabbage, macaroni & tea." While it was cooking, Ewen and Evelyn mounted the horses, Col and Stockings, and went off to find the animals. They discovered the cow, separated from her calf by the pasture fence, and managed to get both of them into the corral. Evelyn would later note in her diary that during lunch, "Mrs. Collins talked for *10*," an indication that Mary must have talked "incessantly," as usual. Evelyn picked some rhubarb for Mary to take home with her, and the three left for Terry: "Mrs. Collins rode Stockings, I Nancy, Ewen Joe. Walked all the way." No further mention was made of the cow and calf.

Cows were allowed to roam freely in Terry, it seems, leading someone to complain in the *Terry Tribune* in February 1913:

One of the greatest nuisances in the town of Terry is the running at large of the town cows and some actions should be taken by the town council looking for a remedy to this evil. It seems to us that when a farmer comes into Terry and wishes to feed his horses in his wagon that he should have the right to do so without the fear that the cows owned by the citizens of Terry will eat more of the feed than the horses.

At the Terry post office, Evelyn received news from England that would threaten to undermine all their plans: "Horrid letter from Wickham's clerk. W. A. Flower refuses to capitalize interest any longer therefore income will be reduced to 200 [pounds] a year. We were oh so blue."

* * *

This was a devastating blow to the young couple. Their financial woes, according to Donna Lucey, had actually begun almost as soon as they moved to Eve Ranch. The owner of the ranch, Henry Tusler, had provided financial backing for Ewen's plan to import two Arabian stallions for breeding as polo ponies. The stallions were kept at Tusler's neighboring ranch, run by his nephew, who was also named Henry Tusler. The Camerons were poorly prepared for the economic realities of this venture, and Ewen and Evelyn soon became enmeshed in a series of financial crises involving bounced checks, angry creditors, and threats of lawsuits. Back in England, Evelyn's cousin, attorney Wickham Flower, was the trustee for her inheritance. They appealed to him for help, but he refused to advance them any money.

Ewen was offered a position managing a polo pony ranch in the Big Horn Mountains in Wyoming, working for Oliver Henry Wallop, son of the Earl of Portsmouth, and a well-known and successful rancher. But Evelyn argued for staying at Eve Ranch, moving to Wyoming only as a last resort. She was able to persuade Ewen that she had come up with some ways to make a bit of money.

On December 2, 1893, she had welcomed a wealthy boarder

named Adams, an Irish friend of her brother Alec, to the ranch. At first it appeared that Adams would invest in the ranch and become a partner in Ewen's polo pony business, but by December 25th of that year, frictions between Adams and Alec had already come to a head. Alec no longer wanted to share his room with Adams, and Adams complained that, "Alec did all sorts of things to annoy him . . ." Evelyn had gotten very angry with her brother and wrote in her diary: "He wants a thorough good thrashing [&] if I were like [our neighbor] Mrs. Kempton he wouldn't be long getting it." The next night she wrote: "Such a child for his years was never seen outside of an idiot." And on January 25, 1894: "Alec & Adams had a 'set to' last night the incentive being Alec taking coal out of his stove after Mr. Adams had put it in! We heard them in our room but didn't interfere. Mr. Adams told Ewen this morn that he knocked Alec down twice, 2nd time onto the bed & gave him a good pummeling. Alec this morn asked Mr. Adams to forgive him!! & also begged Mr. Adams not to tell us." As a result of such incidents, the Camerons would eventually build a guesthouse.

The situation went from bad to worse during the spring of 1894. Adams quickly lost interest in the ranching business and spent much of his time loafing about, not offering to help with daily chores. It's not hard to detect a note of aggravation in Evelyn's entry for April 29: "Out and chopped. Mr. Adams came & watched me . . . He sat in seemingly rather a morose mood on the saw buck smoking his never absent pipe. He has also taken to chewing [tobacco] the last month." Then Adams announced that he would return to Ireland in August. Not only did he fail to invest in the ranch as they had hoped, but now they would not have the benefit of his board and room payments.

Evelyn was also supplementing their income by raising vegetables in her one-acre garden. Alec often gave her a hand, but it was mainly through her own considerable efforts that she grew large amounts of produce, loaded the vegetables into her wagon and delivered them to customers far and wide: to ranches, cook wagons, and even to cowboys at a saloon. One of her steady customers was, of course, Mary Collins.

During his stay at Eve ranch, Adams had talked enthusiastically about cameras and photography. Evelyn decided to take advantage of his expertise and learn as much as she could from him before his departure. This would become her third moneymaking project.

* * *

"F. A. Lisk went down to Terry on Friday especially to see the handsome Arabian stallions recently imported by Capt. E. S. Cameron. Mr. Lisk was very much surprised at their appearance, and declared that they are without exception the prettiest pieces of horseflesh he ever saw. One of them is a slightly dappled iron-gray, 6 years old, weighing 760 pounds, and is 14 1/4 hands high. The other is a mahogany bay, the same age and height, and weighs 800 pounds. There have never been more than half a dozen of these animals brought to this country, and they are almost a curiosity. They are modeled very much after the thoroughbred racer, only Mr. Lisk declares that they far exceed them all in point of beauty. They were imported specially for breeding polo ponies, and are at Henry Tusler's ranch, where he and the captain will keep them."

– News clipping pasted in the front of Evelyn's 1893 diary.

Chapter 7

"Mrs. Collins is gone to Fallon yesterday & is going to live in tents."

TUESDAY, JULY 24, 1894
Arra. about photo outfit. Down to Terry. Got 6 1/4 lbs. beef.
"Lovely. But awful hot wind from South. 106° in shade."

Mr. Adams, the boarder, was about to leave Eve Ranch, so this morning Evelyn got him "to promise to make out a list of photo materials." With his help, she would know just what to order. That night she would write at the top of her diary page: "*Arra.* [arranged] *about photo outfit.*"

Evelyn had already given much thought to learning the art of photography. The year before, when the Camerons had agonized over their financial woes, they contemplated returning to Great Britain and moving to the Orkney Islands, off the coast of Scotland, to study the local wildlife. Evelyn had proposed that she would take photographs to illustrate Ewen's writings on the subject. Another inspiration was L.A. Huffman, a professional photographer with his own studio in Miles City. She would buy a photo from him the next year. (He would later buy prints and negatives from her, praising her work highly.)

Many British expatriates had brought cameras with them to Montana, notably the Kodak, with flexible rolls of film, which had come on the market in 1888. Mr. Adams, however, was partial to the dry-plate glass negative process, so it was on his recommendation that she ordered this type of camera, although she did not record the make or style. Mr. Adams had not brought his own camera with him, so he was excited to make the trip to the Terry railroad depot on August 13 to pick up Evelyn's new camera. The next evening he would show her how to change the plates, "Great business to exclude all the light, moon in full blast."

Before lunch, Evelyn picked "a big pan full of string beans and some cucumbers." She and Mr. Adams rode into town on horseback, with Mr. Adams carrying the beans. They were on their way to see Mrs. Collins when they met Mr. Coggshall, who was going to Miles City that night and planning to visit the Camerons the next day. (Mr. Coggshall was a successful local rancher who had helped out the Camerons financially in 1893. They had mortgaged their ranch to him to keep creditors off their backs.) Evelyn discovered that "Mrs. Collins [has] gone to Fallon yesterday & is going to live in tents."

They were able to barter the beans with a Mrs. Watkins for six and a quarter pounds of beef. The meat was handed up to Evelyn as she sat on the back of her horse. "Nancy didn't mind," Evelyn noted in her diary, perhaps referring to the odor of the fresh beef, which she feared would bother her skittish horse. Mr. Adams waited in town for the late mail while she rode back alone, arriving at the ranch at six o'clock.

* * *

SUNDAY, JULY 29, 1894
<u>Mr. Adams early to Fallon. Ewen & I, 9.30 started for Fallon. Shipping & Collins.</u>
Arose 4.40. Glorious West breeze.
   Planning to spend a full day in Fallon at the roundup, Evelyn got

Meetings With Mrs. Collins

up especially early to complete her chores. She milked the cows while Ewen spent a frustrating hour bringing in a calf from the pasture. "The little brute would stay & run to [the] thickest brush." Was it, perhaps, the Collins calf? After breakfast at seven thirty, the Camerons set off for Fallon on horseback "round by the Terry road." On the way they saw "6 turkey buzzards eating at the entrails of a calf killed by Keliman's wagon. Got to Fallon 11.15. Went first to Mrs. Lewis' shacks where was Mrs. Kempton & Mrs. Collins sitting."

* * *

Mrs. Kempton was a neighboring rancher, a half-Indian woman whose impressive bearing, and strong personality, led Evelyn to believe that she would put up with no nonsense. Evelyn had earlier referred to Mrs. Kempton in her diary when she wrote of her brother Alec: "He wants a thorough good thrashing [&] if I were like Mrs. Kempton he wouldn't be long getting it."

Mrs. Kempton had an interesting lineage. She was born Marie (or Mariah) Gerry. Her father, Elbridge Gerry, was reputedly the nephew of Elbridge Gerry, a signer of the Declaration of Independence (while governor of Massachusetts in 1811, his activities gave rise to the term "gerrymander"). He had left home as a young man, joined a Sioux Indian tribe, and shared their nomadic life. Marie was one of the four children he had with Flora, the first of his two Sioux wives. Marie married wealthy cattleman James Kempton, a Civil War veteran who had brought two herds of cattle to eastern Montana from the Northwest to establish a ranch, eventually settling near Terry.

Evelyn had picked up a few frontier skills from Mrs. Kempton. This procedure for tanning hides she recorded in her diary on May 28, 1894:

> Mrs. Kempton . . . had been making gloves from her own tanned hides, beautifully tanned. . . . She soaks the skin in the creek till soft then scrapes all the hair off. . . . 2nd, 2 table spoonfulls of lard or suet melted [she] rubs in the hide, [&] leaves it for few days, 3rdly, [she] washes the grease out in

lukewarm soap sudded water, [the skin is] then pulled & rubbed dry by 2 people. Not at all difficult to do she says, certainly the result is worthy of some labour.

Mrs. Kempton was also the source of some dubious-sounding medical remedies. Since the only doctor was in Miles City, most pioneers were willing to give anything a try. Strangest of all is this cure for frostbite, entered in the back of Evelyn's 1896 diary:

Mr. Kempton once had his feet so severely frost bitten that 3 doctors said he would die if they were not cut off. Mr. Kempton was determined not to have them amputated. An old "darkie" woman happened to call for his mother's washing. She saw his feet & at once said they could be saved. Her receipt being *baked common white turnips*, the inside (pulp) of the rhind applied quite hot as a poltice to the frozen parts. . . . For the first 5 days the poltice had to be renewed 3 or 4 times, the very wet pulp being entirely absorbed by the feet. At the end of 5 days the moisture no longer became absorbed but remained in the poltice. In about 18 days the skin of the foot came off entirely like a mocassin. "Darkie" then advised very tight slippers or boots to prevent feet spreading. After the skin came off, the feet were a bright puffy red colour & when stood upon felt as if they would burst. [The] feet cracked down soles but finally became as well as ever through this treatment. *Related March 8th '96 by Mr. Kempton.*

In 1890, the Kempton's son Berney had became famous in the "Doc" Carver Wild America show, demonstrating his roping and riding skills. The troupe traveled to Hungary, Poland, Russia, and even Australia, where he boasted of being the first cowboy to rope a kangaroo.

Mrs. Kempton was a close friend of Mrs. Collins. Her granddaughter Bernice, daughter of Berney and his first wife Flora Kasper, would one day wed Mary Collins' grandson, Lynn Ingersoll.

* * *

Meetings With Mrs. Collins

Mr. and Mrs. J. B. Kempton, close friends of Evelyn Cameron and Mary Collins. *Cameron photograph, courtesy of the Prairie County Museum, Terry, Montana.(Box X, Neg. 55, EC41)*

Colleen Elizabeth Carter

Dr. W. F. ("Doc") Carver's Wild America. Standing, left to right: Billy Garnet, Painted Horse, Jim Marsh, Berney Kempton. Seated, left to right: He Crow, Mrs. Black Bear, Black Bear, 1890-1891. Berney Kempton's daughter Bernice married Mrs. Collins' grandson, Lynn Ingersoll. *Photograph courtesy of the Prairie County Museum, Terry, Montana. (Box XVIII, Neg. 7, EC42)*

Evelyn left Mrs. Lewis' shacks with Mrs. Collins, and walked over to the three tents Mary had set up as living quarters and cook tents. It was time to prepare the midday meal, and Evelyn wanted to see firsthand how Mrs. Collins managed this daunting job. Offering to lend a hand, she "helped dish up & wait, 10 or 13 altogether, 2 tables full. I did all washing & wiping up for her." It would no doubt have amused her aristocratic friends in Miles City to see her so engaged.

Mary's cooking tents provided an important source of income for her. Other women, less reputable, apparently found employment at the Fallon roundup. On September 11, Evelyn went into Terry, where she heard that, "a woman [was] killed by a man (cowboy) at Donelly's indecent shacks at Fallon yesterday."

Later in the afternoon, Ewen and Evelyn went to the stockyards

Meetings With Mrs. Collins

and, as before, chatted with the local ranchers while they watched the cowboys load cattle onto the railroad cars. At about five o'clock, they "made for home," an hour and a half ride. Waiting for Evelyn at home were her usual evening chores, plus a special supper at eight thirty for their guest, Mr. Coggshall, of "Beef croquettes, potatoes, sweet corn, squash, cold rice pudding." Evelyn didn't get to bed until eleven fifteen. "Mr. Coggshall slept [in] Adam's room. Mr. Adams sleeps out[side] always now."

* * *

Subsequent diary entries for 1894 reveal the full extent of Mrs. Collins' stay at the Fallon roundup. Sunday, August 26, was Evelyn's birthday, though no festivities were planned. She and Alec rode horseback to Fallon, Alec carrying the string beans, cucumbers, and tomatoes, and Evelyn carrying two cabbages. Their boarder Adams had returned to Ireland and Evelyn remarked, "It is quite a rest to be without Mr. Adams." At Fallon, she "sat with Mrs. Collins. Drank water & ate cookies. She walked with me to Laneys no one at home." Later, as Evelyn and Alec rode home, they were accompanied part of the way by a drunken "cowpuncher." (The term "cowpuncher" refers to the cowboy's task of prodding cattle in the cars with a pole to prevent them from lying down.)

The following Sunday, September 2, Evelyn "dug potatoes #14, plucked about 8 1/2 bushels of tomatoes, cucumbers young & ready for sweet pickles, 8 cabbages, 2 cauliflowers, beets, Alec got butter beans & green beans." They loaded the produce into the wagon and drove to Fallon. Evelyn sold cabbages and beets to a chuck wagon cook near Fallon, and tomatoes to a Mrs. Van. In Fallon, she went to see Mrs. Collins, "who gave us beef pie & cake to take home! Gave her vegetables." A man at the nearby saloon bought four cabbages, and she sold the rest of the tomatoes to Mrs. Laney. They met Ewen at the roundup. He and their neighbor Hamlin had driven a group of horses to Fallon the night before and had quite a difficult time loading them into the freight car for shipment. For some reason, Ewen was "very mad" at Evelyn and slept in Mr. Adam's room that night.

Evelyn's next trip was about three weeks later, on September 22. The new boarder, Mr. Colley, helped her sack up 200 pounds of potatoes. Evelyn also harvested cabbages, squash, rutabagas, and tomatoes. The wagon, she estimated, had a load weighing about 1000 pounds. After lunch, Evelyn, Mr. Colley, and Alec rode to Fallon. While Evelyn was busy selling her vegetables, "Mr. Ferdon came up & asked me to do him a favor! viz: to accept a fine 4 yr. heifer [with a] broken shoulder (offered 15$ for her but [he] would rather I took her for nothing) awfully kind." They found Mr. Lewis, who promised to butcher it, and they all rode about a mile to where the injured heifer was. "She got up on fight, Alec went to get revolver but cowboy (Williams –X—) came roped & threw her. Offered Williams $1 [he] refused but got him to take it to treat others with. Lewis cut her up. He was very slow. . . . Mr. Colley took 3 photos with Kodak of heifer." They delivered a forequarter to Ferdon "for his trouble." Evelyn noted in her diary that, " Mrs. Collins came out with pie & Mrs. Lewis with cake & tea."

* * *

Evelyn's diary recorded a number of additional contacts with Mrs.Collins in 1894:

March 23: "Filled 2 sack with a 100 lbs each & with the other 100 lbs I had sorted some time ago made 300 lbs. . . . Ewen and I were going to ride down to Terry but Braley came up with some hay from Kempton, so E went down to Terry with him & he took the lbs 300 of taters to Mrs. Collins."

March 24: "I went to Mrs. Collins got $1 from her on potatoe acct. & gave it to Mr. A to send bob cat with." [Probably for the taxidermist.]

March 26: "(Mrs. Collins introduced me to Mr. Bogard in the depot)"

April 1: "Went over to Mrs. Collins she paid me the balance on potatoes $5."

November 28: "Mrs. Furnish came out to meet me [at the post

Meetings With Mrs. Collins

office], she finally gave me all the mail which 1/2 filled a gunny sack. I went up to see her baby, saw two people, the woman expressed her dislike very strongly to camping out. Spoke to Drew, Mrs. Collins. Went to store: got yeast cakes, 5 1/2 lbs bacon, tin plate for Mrs. Collins, & 3 tins condensed milk."

December 9: "Went up to see Mrs. Furnish who was with the baby upstairs. Got cold (baby). No mail for me. Mrs. Collins down in kitchen." [The Furnish baby, born in August, seems to have been the object of much concern. Evelyn had first seen it when it was three weeks old: "She has got such a wee bit of a baby . . . smallest ever seen." Perhaps Mary was lending a hand in the kitchen to allow Mrs. Furnish to care for her sick infant. It's also possible that Mary took over the post office temporarily, giving rise to a later memory that she was once a postmistress, as her obituary states.]

In the back of her 1894 diary Evelyn noted sales of vegetables to Mrs. Collins. In addition to the three hundred pounds of potatoes sold on March 23, Mary had ordered another sixty pounds in August, and sales of cabbages on the fifth, twelfth, and twenty-sixth of August.

Chapter 8

"Drew caught his wife in an indecent way in Miles City."

SATURDAY, FEBRUARY 9, 1895
Pretty big woolen wash—that's it. Mr. C & Ewen to Terry. E. had a bath.
Frosty. Lovely. Afternoon snowed thickly. Snow stop.

On this day, Evelyn noted that the temperature was minus four degrees at eight o'clock in the morning, and minus two degrees at seven thirty in the evening. She arose at seven fifteen, lit the fires, milked the cows, and cleaned their stalls. She prepared a substantial breakfast of "bacon & po. [poached] eggs, beef, olives, fried tatoes, porridge, cream, toast," and swept the house while she waited for water to heat in the big boiler. At 12:25 she began her "big woolen wash."

At two thirty, Ewen rode to Terry with Mr. Colley, the wealthy new border who had come to stay after the departure of Mr. Adams in August. When Evelyn finished her washing an hour later, she had to decide what she would be able to accomplish, with the rest of the hot water, in the few remaining hours of the afternoon. She ended up washing the "skirts" [baseboards], "which were pine besmoked very black." She also "tried the rubber window cleaner but too many corners for it. Only good I think for porch."

In Terry, meanwhile, Ewen and Colley "sampled whiskies and brandies at Drew's saloon. Drew told Ewen he had $130 worth of beer in barrels spoilt by freezing!" The loss of such a sum, representing three to four months' pay for the former cowboy, was merely the latest in a series of disasters to befall Drew, the Cameron's former neighbor. In April 1893, Drew had moved from Miles City with his young wife and son Jack to work as a cowboy on the Tusler Ranch, a short walk from Eve Ranch. Mrs. Drew cooked for the ranch, and kept an eye on their three-year-old son Jack, described by Evelyn as "fearfully disobedient" and an "awfully willful child," who "actually swears like a man."

The isolation of pioneer existence and the scarcity of female companionship had brought the two women together, and Mrs. Drew often depended on Evelyn for advice. On June 27, 1894, there was a medical emergency: "Little Jack had gotten hold of a bottle in stable thinking it whisky (which he loves!) & had drunk some. I rode Andy on Ewen's saddle full tilt up there. Mrs. Drew was with the child in bedroom. He looked well, nice colour, lively, no pains. . . . Made mustard & warm water, [&] by dint of a lot of coaxing he swallowed very few drops. Held him & tried to force some down."

The Panic of 1893, leading to the bankruptcy of the Northern Pacific Railroad and a general railroad strike, had a disastrous impact on ranching in Montana. Henry Tusler was forced to let Drew go. On August 17, 1894, the family had driven out to Eve Ranch in their buggy. "[Jack] had big sores on his face & looks very pale [from scarlet fever]. Mrs. Drew looks pale," Evelyn had remarked. "Drew says [there's] no pleasure to be had for a poor man."

Evelyn saw the family again in Terry on August 31, and offered, most likely without Ewen's enthusiastic consent, to let little Jack spend the night at Eve Ranch: "Drove little Jack home with us as Drew [is] coming up in morning to bandage up the ponies' tails for the journey [to England]. Supper 7.20. Milked after. Jack hung on to me the whole time. He is a dear little boy, certainly he is not behaving like an enfant terrible as I expected he would. I slept on floor, Ewen slept in Adams' room & Jack in our bed, as Ewen is afraid of infection from scarlet fever, so I slept on floor."

On November 28, 1894, Evelyn observed that things had gone from bad to worse for the Drew family: "Drew caught his wife in an indecent way in Miles City. They are separated. Drew is building a saloon in Terry."

Mrs. Drew, a competent dressmaker, who also took in laundry (shirts for fifteen cents apiece) and tanned skins to eke out a living for herself and her son, had hopes of becoming a milliner in nearby Glendive. But this did not go as planned, and she apparently turned to Mrs. Collins for help. When Ewen and Colley returned from their visit to Drew's saloon, Ewen mentioned to Evelyn that the "Drews keep hotel in Mrs. Collin's house & she lives (Mrs. C) with them."

The live-and-let-live attitude of the early 1880s frontier had by then given way to a more judgmental "Eastern" sensibility. The scandal surrounding Mrs. Drew's circumstances caused the "polite society" of Terry to shun her. But this seems not to have mattered to Mary, nor to Evelyn, who both supported her in the face of widespread ostracism. As Donna Lucey notes:

> Evelyn . . . had no patience with the gossip and petty cruelty of small-town life, and in May 1895 when one of the local busybodies invited Mrs. Cameron into her house to visit, Evelyn made her sympathies quite plain: "I thanked her saying I was going to call on Mrs. Drew. This must have made her talk scandal by the hour after." She found Mrs. Drew "pale," but undoubtedly pleased to see her old neighbor.

Evelyn hired Mrs. Drew to do some sewing for her. On August 5, 1896, she reported: "I paid Mrs. Drew $10 for doing my dress making & skirts altered to style & divided skirt awfully well made & hangs beautifully." Evelyn frequently borrowed Ewen's trousers for long horseback rides, convinced that riding astride was safer than riding on the more traditional British sidesaddle, so she referred to her new split skirt as a "safety skirt." This divided skirt was probably modeled on a "California riding costume" that Evelyn had ordered from Chicago for $100. But the next summer, when she wore it in the streets of Miles City, a town famous for its rowdy saloons and bordellos, it caused a stir—and even a threat of arrest.

The prejudice Evelyn encountered against her split skirt originally derived from the biblical injunction, "The woman shall not wear that which pertaineth unto a man," (*Deuteronomy* 22:5) but many women on the frontier, where they often did a man's work, embraced the loose trousers covered by a short skirt, called "Bloomers," designed in 1851 by Amelia Bloomer. Evelyn's divided skirt was essentially a pair of culottes with a panel that could be buttoned across the front to give the appearance of a normal skirt. It did not take long for Montana women, even in Miles City, to welcome this innovation.

When her skirt began to wear out, Evelyn found a way to extend its life. On December 6, 1896, she wrote: "Set to patch my old divided skirt [with] leather put on inside the legs. Took me till chore time to finish one side & commence on the other."

* * *

"Understand those who misunderstand thee. Be fair to those who are unfair to thee. Be just & merciful to those whom thou wouldst like to hate. Forgive & thou shalt be forgiven."

— Written inside the front cover of Evelyn's 1902 diary.

Chapter 9

"Ewen & I had a 'difference.'"

MONDAY, APRIL 8, 1895
<u>Rather full day. Manured garden. Drove to Terry in wagon.</u>
Glorious day. 72° in shade 1 p.m. Breeze.

Despite the beautiful morning, the day started out badly for Evelyn. There were extra hired hands at the ranch to feed, adding to Evelyn's usual workload. Getting up at 6:20, she milked, "cleaned whole stable out," and at eight fifteen, served breakfast to the "boys."

Ewen was ill and peevish. An unexplained argument kept Ewen and Evelyn from eating breakfast together: "Ewen & I had a 'difference,' ate mine alone. Ewen ate some later." She washed up after the men had eaten and went outside with Alec to work in the garden. But here, too, she met with frustration: "Got out seeds to plant. Alec wheeled manure from pile in garden (old rotted) onto s.w. corner, but too frozen to dig in so left it on top for today to thaw out. Sewed some cabbage seed in box."

Later, Ewen decided to drive down to Terry in the wagon, and sent her out to harness up the team. "Kaddy [Cady] Scott and L. Braley [the Cameron's hired hands] arrive, they went in." Evelyn served lunch, got dressed, and finally left with Ewen at about three o'clock.

Whatever had caused their "difference" in the morning had likely left Evelyn in an unsociable mood. She made the entire trip without getting out of the wagon, likely to discourage time-consuming "jabbing" (jabbering) at their stops in town. After a stop at the post office, Evelyn stayed in the wagon while they paid a brief visit to Mrs. Collins. "I didn't get out [the] whole time," Evelyn remarked.

She picked up a "box from Miles [City] of 12 dozen eggs," and placed them on one of the seats, where Ewen accidentally sat on top of them. "They made a great mess in wagon." Fifteen-year-old Mary Kempton asked them for a ride home. When they stopped at the Kempton ranch to let her off, Evelyn "didn't descend. Mrs. Kempton came out, [and] jabbed."

That night after supper, Evelyn and Alec picked through the box of eggs, rescuing and cleaning what they could, a process that "took [a] long time." She did not get to bed until 11:35.

* * *

TUESDAY, APRIL 9, 1895
<u>Stitched at Ewen's clothes. Ewen & I drove to Terry. 13 [Ranch] burnt down we heard</u>.
Dull. Cold East wind.

The following day found Ewen still irritable, but Evelyn, in a more sympathetic mood, wrote: "Ewen hasn't felt well last two days—nervous debility." She milked the cows, cleaned the stable, groomed four horses, and "mended buckskin breeches & put numerous buttons on," which kept her busy until lunch at one thirty. For the second day in a row, the Camerons made the trip to Terry. Ewen helped her harness the wagon team, and they set off at three o'clock. Their dog had earlier followed Alec up to the Tusler Ranch, and as they drove by, "Bruin came running to us. Ewen thrashed him."

Again they went to see Mrs. Collins, who presented the Camerons with a rooster and two hens. One of the hens escaped: "Had to run one hen down. Gibson's boy did [it] for us." They also picked up a "bit [of] shoulder beef" from Mrs. Jordan, and some oil and wagon grease from another merchant.

They were home by 6:20. This evening, after what she called "foal and cow chores," Evelyn put together a supper of "croquettes, macaroni, mashed potato, light Madeira cookies, cream, jam, coffee, tea," which they ate at 8:10.

* * *

"Strive daily & hourly to be <u>calm</u>; to stop yourself forcibly & recall your mind to a sense of what you are, where you are going, & whither you ought to be tending. This is most painful, discipline, but most wholesome. M.S. 1842 C.K."

—Written in the front of Evelyn's 1902 diary.

Chapter 10

"She gave me her family tree & experiences generally after leaving old Oireland."

MONDAY, APRIL 29, 1895
<u>Got up team. Drove to Terry. Mr. Colley, Alec & I. Evening developed films.</u> *Dull. East wind. No rain felt very much like it.*

The new boarder, Mr. Colley, like Mr. Adams before him, was an experienced photographer. He had brought with him a small Kodak camera that used roll film, which Ewen greatly admired. Evelyn, however, still preferred the quality of the prints made from her large glass negatives. Colley was happy to help her with her early photographic attempts, and the two had stayed up till 12:10 the night before, developing the day's negative plates.

On April 28, as a joke, Evelyn had tried to photograph her brother Alec as a hanged man. "It struck me to get Alec & hang him up with the pack saddle surcingle [a band that goes around the horse's body] fixed under his arms . . . we improvised a detached short piece of rope to go round his neck for a noose, otherwise he hung of course entirely from the surcingle." She wrote that Alec had "consented without a murmur (much to my surprise)."At this point in her development as a photographer she was reliant on Mr. Colley's expertise, and frustrated by the poor outcomes of her efforts. "The result of my work is experience—nothing more," she wrote that night. Today she complained that the previous night's work had left her "rather weary. Headache all day of a subdued nature."

After morning chores and a breakfast of "eggs, porridge, coffee, hot buttered toast," Evelyn went out to the pasture to find the horses, carrying bridles and a feedbag. She set off in the wagon at 12:20 with Alec and Mr. Colley. She noticed that the "horses went very well. They seemed to feel the new grass." When they reached Terry, they tied up the wagon at Stith's hardware store and went to Scott's, where she paid the thirty cents she owed them for butter.

Evelyn left Alec and her boarder to their own devices and went alone to see Mrs. Collins. It had been quite a while since Evelyn and Mary had enjoyed a long chat. "She made me eat eggs, pancakes & cup of tea, both excellent." During this visit Evelyn would learn more about the eccentric Irishwoman. "She gave me her family tree & experiences generally after leaving old Oireland."

* * *

The family lore is sketchy when it comes to details of Mary's life. So far, the earliest document I have found is a marriage record dated January 5, 1856, from St. Patrick's Church in Union Springs, New York. There, at the age of twenty-three, she married Patrick Collins, twenty. Both had emigrated from Ireland. The entry is hard to read, and written in Latin; Patrick's name is actually written as "Cullin." Mary's father is recorded as Hugo McMahon, and her mother as Mary Hughes.

It may never be possible to trace the young Mary Bridgett McMahon back to the Emerald Isle. But, in spite of the faint document trail, it is possible to make informed speculations about her life, as well as the circumstances under which she left Ireland. Mary was born there, most likely in 1833. Because of the close connection between Irish family names and particular places in Ireland, Mary's family, the McMahons, may have come from County Clare, on the west coast of Ireland, or from County Monaghan, where a smaller number of McMahons resided, but in fact she could have come from any part of the country.

Cecil Woodham-Smith, in his book *The Great Hunger*, describes the average Irish-Catholic family in the west of Ireland as having been extremely poor, living in small stone hovels with little or no furniture. In such dwellings, pigs often slept inside with the family, and they all survived on a yearly harvest of potatoes from a plot of rented land, supplemented with buttermilk, and a few "green crops" from a little vegetable garden. In western Ireland there was little employment for wages.

The Great Potato Famine hit hardest in the western counties. William Bennett, a Quaker philanthropist, wrote: "It was my impression that *one-fourth* of those we saw were in a *dying state*, beyond the reach of any relief that could now be afforded; and many more would follow."

The Famine lasted from 1845 to 1849, leaving almost a million people dead, many thrown into pits and covered with quicklime. It's estimated that another 1,600,000 Irish immigrated to the United States during the period 1847 to 1854. According to family lore, Mary McMahon was among the many famine refugees who left for America. When the migration grew to a deluge in 1847, after the second potato crop failure, Mary would have been fifteen, old enough to have made the journey alone, perhaps leaving on a ship from Galway, a popular point of departure from the western counties. The Irish immigration differed from other ethnic migrations in that more women than men took part, primarily lone, single "girls."

Like other Irish immigrants during the famine, Mary left her home in order to survive. The Irish had suffered periodic famines over the course of their history, but nothing as catastrophic as the Great Famine, one of the worst disasters of the nineteenth century. It left survivors with a lifetime of emotional pain and anger. Mary must have watched family, friends, and neighbors starve to death, or fall victim to one of the terrible diseases: "black fever," "bloody flux," "famine dropsy," or cholera. Perhaps her family was among those brutally evicted by their landlord, an act that was considered a "death sentence." She had to choose—either to stay, and likely die of starvation, or to risk the arduous journey to America.

Mary was one of the fortunate ones who escaped, and survived. She may have been among the groups of orphaned female children sent to America during the worst years of the famine, to spare the expense of their upkeep in the poorhouse. These young women were described as of a "clean, healthy condition," and would readily find employment in America. The cheapest way to transport these pauper children would have been in the holds of Irish ships, such as the timber ships that carried cargo between Canada and New Brunswick and Irish Ports. These ships had never been designed to carry passengers, so ship owners, eager to earn fares from desperate famine victims, hastily installed berths and took on meager provisions totally inadequate for the voyage.

To reach America, emigrants risked their lives on the dangerous 3,000-mile Atlantic crossing, which took as little as a month, but usually much longer. Many succumbed to disease or starvation at sea—giving rise to the term "coffin ships"—and many more died upon arrival in North America.

Chances are good that Mary's ship entered a Canadian port, since a high percentage of immigrants who later found their way to the Midwest had arrived through Canada. From there she would have headed south, crossing into the United States, either by boat, on foot, or by other means of transportation.

Had she arrived in the port of New York, she would more likely have settled in one of the large Northeastern cities, along with the vast majority of Irish exiles, and might never have ended up on the shores of Lake Cayuga, in western New York State.

In the early part of the nineteenth century, thousands of Irish Catholics had established well-traveled immigrant routes through Canada to the United States. In the early 1820s, the Erie Canal offered employment to Irish men, and after the canal opened in 1828, many of them found jobs as laborers and settled in towns along the canal and its many branches. Such towns later became magnets for immigrants escaping the famine, particularly those who arrived through Canada. It was in one of these towns that Mary most likely met Patrick Collins.

They were married on January 5, 1856, in Union Springs, a rural town on the eastern shore of Lake Cayuga, one of the Finger Lakes in western New York. In 1879 it was described in Elliot Storke's *The History of Cayuga County, 1789-1879* as:

> Beautifully situated on the shore of the lake . . . Its regularly laid out and handsomely shaded streets, with its tasty cottages and ornate dwellings just visible through the luxuriant foliage, present a pleasing picture as viewed from the lake, which, with the little island of Frontenac, that solitary gem of the western lakes, three-fourths of a mile distant, presents an equally picturesque spectacle.

Upon her arrival, Mary may have settled into one of the "shantytowns," derisively called "paddy town" or "Irish town," that cropped up everywhere during the peak of immigration to accommodate the flood of newcomers. The presence in Union Springs of a Catholic Church named St. Patrick's indicates a significant Irish Catholic population. The parish created a safe haven for immigrants, the community and church providing a degree of protection against a hostile, prejudiced citizenry who thought of the newcomers as a backward, uncivilized lot.

Irish men, in particular, were portrayed in illustrations of the time as less than human, with apelike faces. They had a reputation for drunkenness and violence. Single men worked at the most dangerous unskilled and semiskilled jobs, such as the building, upkeep, and operation of the canals, reservoirs, turnpikes, and railroads. Married men with families were more likely to gravitate to grimy mill towns such as Lowell and Lawrence, Massachusetts, where factories employed parents and their children.

Historian Hasia Diner, in her book *Erin's Daughters in America*, describes the unique qualities that made the Irish immigrant women more successful than the men, and more successful than women of any other immigrant group. Her exploration of the opportunities available at the time offers insight into the choices

Colleen Elizabeth Carter

Mary made.

If she had settled in one of the large urban areas such as Boston or New York, Mary might have found herself toiling in sweatshop conditions in the garment industry. Such employment offered the worst opportunities for economic advancement. Instead, Mary found herself in the most enviable situation a young Irish girl could have hoped for—a job as a domestic servant, perhaps in one of the "ornate dwellings" of Union Springs. As a domestic, Mary would have lived in the house of her employers and shared their food, leaving her with few living expenses. Working in an American home would have given her a glimpse of American middle-class manners and values, and it would have provided the opportunity to improve her English.

The workdays were long and hard; the girls were frequently subjected to prejudice and verbal abuse from their employers, yet Irish girls aspired to domestic service above all other types of employment. The great availability of these jobs was the very reason so many had come to America. Native-born American girls scorned domestic work, as did women of all other European ethnic immigrant groups, but Irish women had a special affinity for it. As a servant Mary would have earned substantially more than mill workers and textile workers, and by frugal saving could have accumulated a tidy sum by the time she married.

Irish girls arrived in America without the household skills that would qualify them for work in wealthy homes. Although they were in great demand as domestics, they had to start out in the most unskilled positions and work their way up. Local "Intelligence Offices" connected Irish girls with employers, after making each girl sign a "Testimonial of Moral Conduct." They often dismayed their middle- and upper-class employers with their clumsiness, personal habits, and impudence, but many learned quickly and became highly esteemed and trusted by their employers.

Mary may have worked in a hotel, thus acquiring the knowledge and business skills that would one day provide her with economic independence. During this time she would have mastered the workings of an American kitchen, and learned to prepare the simple but robust cuisine favored by Americans of that era. It was a radical transformation for the Irish peasant girl, whose prior cooking experiences were likely limited to potatoes, cabbages, and a bit of bacon cooked over an open fire. Throughout her life, Mary would refer to herself as a "housekeeper."

Young Irish women knew the risks of marrying an Irish man. Gender segregation and hostility were characteristic of Irish marriages in both Ireland and America in the nineteenth century. Men carried on most of their activities in the male sphere, at work and in the pub, while women spent their days in the company of children and other women. Men were part of a proud patriarchal culture. Irish wives, however, were not subservient, and usually controlled the finances of the family, carefully doling out the husband's pub money to ensure that their children could eat. In America, relationships became even more fragile as husbands saw their wives gain more economic power and self-confidence—and the frequent result was desertion. Wives who were not abandoned often found themselves widowed at an early age as a result of the dangerous work most Irish men performed.

Most young Irish women in Mary's position would have been extremely reluctant to marry and give up the hard-won economic power they had achieved. In fact, many postponed marriage until they reached their thirties or forties, sometimes choosing never to marry. Back in Ireland, most women had been doomed to poverty and a life of child rearing and housework. The male-dominated church was unsympathetic to women's needs and helped perpetuate the status quo.

In spite of these drawbacks, Mary became a married woman, at the age of twenty-three, and as such her working life would be restricted to the home. Her husband Patrick was even younger than she, only twenty, and unable to sign his own name. In 1864 a Civil War recruiting officer would give his description: "This soldier has hazel eyes, black hair, dark complexion, is 5 feet 7 inches." His appearance would have presented a contrast to his wife, who is remembered as tall and red-haired.

A common dream, fueled by "Western Fever" may have forged their union—but this was an unusual dream for the Potato Famine Irish. Their agricultural experience was limited to a potato patch.

They had little money, and many were ill or weakened from their ordeals. It's estimated that less than ten percent of Irish immigrants became farmers and pioneers.

Mary's carefully hoarded savings would likely have provided much of the capital for this bold step. The couple stayed in Union Springs long enough to bear a child the following November. Mary gave her oldest daughter her own name, followed by "Madore," and would call her "Mamie," or "Maude."

While other ethnic immigrant groups, such as Norwegians and Germans, benefited from organized migrations and established colonies, the Irish had fewer such advantages—they were, for the most part, on their own. Minnesota became a state in 1858, opening up new lands for sale, and immigrants from Sweden, Norway, and Denmark began arriving. The Irish arrived in smaller numbers, and sent letters to their compatriots back east describing the wonders of the new state. With America in the grip of an economic downturn, to go west must have been an attractive choice.

By 1860, a network of railroad lines had spread from the Atlantic coast cities as far as Illinois, eastern Iowa, and Wisconsin, carrying migrating families to the edge of the frontier. Although Patrick and Mary could have traveled west by train, the town of Union Springs lay close by the Erie Canal. The canal's heyday as a transportation route for westward migration had come and gone, but canal travel could still have been the cheapest and most convenient means for them. The poorest immigrants took the "lineboats," which were pulled by horse or mule at a rate of about two miles per hour. They were overcrowded, and sleeping berths were often shared with bedbugs, lice, roaches, and fleas. From Buffalo, steamboat passage through the Great Lakes may have taken them to Milwaukee, from whence they could have traveled by railroad to La Crosse, Minnesota, on the Mississippi River, fifty miles from their destination.

They were in Minnesota during the 1860 Federal Census. Mary, using the name Bridgett Collins, and her four-year-old daughter Mary, were residing in Rock Dell, Olmstead County. Patrick is listed at the home of John Pierson, a neighboring farmer. Perhaps he was working as a farm hand, or maybe visiting. Sarah

Meetings With Mrs. Collins

Collins was born on December 2, 1860.

In 1861, Patrick filed for a land patent in High Forest, Olmstead County.

Two more children were born there: James F. in 1863, and Rose, "Rosie," in 1866. Mary avoided typically Irish names for her younger children, instead choosing ones that sounded more "American." "Rose" was an especially loved name during the Victorian era. All of her surviving children would eventually "marry out," choosing non-Irish mates. (Although James' wife had an Irish grandmother.)

Mary Collins had already told Evelyn some things about her life in Minnesota—about the hard times during the Civil War, and about her abusive husband, who deserted the family in 1870. Mary had determinedly found a way to make ends meet for herself and her four young children, most likely by taking in boarders and laundry.

During those years on her own, she suffered a great loss. In the High Forest cemetery stands a slender monument, over six feet tall and topped by an Irish Cross. There, two years after her husband's departure, Mary buried her daughter Sarah, who had died of a "hemorrhage of the lung," possibly from pneumonia. (The obituary states: "In the village of High Forest, October 14th, 1872, SARAH E. COLLINS, in the twelfth year of her age.") Sarah's tombstone towers above the surrounding grave markers, the size and quality certainly representing an economic sacrifice. Its Irish Cross is a link to past sorrows in the land Mary had left behind. She bore this loss alone, and declared that fact in an unusual inscription on the tombstone: "Erected by her mother."

A few months after Sarah's death, Minnesota was hit with a series of sudden and fierce blizzards, causing widespread pain and hardship, worse than the homesteaders had ever experienced on the plains. The first, on January 7, 1873, blew continuously for three days, with the temperature down to 40 below zero. There followed another in early March, and again in mid-April. Frostbite was common, domestic animals froze to death, and families struggled to keep themselves warm.

The following year brought the Financial Panic of 1873, and

then came the epic grasshopper plague of 1874, followed by four years of grasshopper infestations. These were years of distress and hunger for settlers. Finally, in 1877, the grasshoppers became infected with a parasite and died off. That year, the economy began to improve.

By June 1880, according to the federal census, Mary had moved to the Village of Grand Meadow, with Rose, age thirteen, and James, age sixteen. She took in laundry to make a frugal living, while her son worked as a laborer. Her oldest child, Mary Madore, was married to a man named Charles Auten, and they also lived in Grand Meadow, along with their children, William, three years of age, and Sarah, one year old. Our family accounts maintain that Mary left Minnesota in 1880, when Rose, her youngest, was fourteen years old. Her son James (my great-grandfather), a restless and ambitious lad, then set off on his own, working as a farm hand.

Pension documents for Patrick Collins indicate that after leaving his family, and following his arrest on charges of bigamy, he wandered about working as a farm laborer. His wanderings occasionally brought him into contact with Mary. In 1880, apparently feeling threatened, Mary saw her opportunity to escape. With only her daughter Rose to care for, she was about to embark on another great adventure. In fact, the next chapter of her life would thrust her into the midst of one of the great adventures of the American West. By crossing the ninety-eighth meridian, the eastern boundary of what was once called the Great American Desert, she was casting her fate with others who sought a new life on the Great Plains.

* * *

In 1864, President Abraham Lincoln signed a charter for the planning and building of a railroad to follow the route taken by Lewis and Clark during their brilliantly executed expedition to the Pacific Ocean in 1804-06. In 1870, groundbreaking ceremonies took place for the Northern Pacific Railroad near Duluth, Minnesota. The Financial Panic of 1873, triggered by the railroad invest-

Tombstone of Mary's daughter, Sarah Collins, 1860-1872, in High Forest, Minnesota. The words "Erected by her mother" appear at the top of the marker, partly obscured by lichen. *Collection of author.*

ors' financial difficulties, brought work to a halt for four years, but then it slowly started up again. In the winter of 1879, crews were able to cross the Missouri River by laying down ties directly on the frozen surface of the river. On November 10, 1880, the Dakota/Montana boundary was reached, and in December, track laying stopped for the winter about thirty miles east of Glendive, Montana.

Historian David Laskin writes about this winter, known as the "Snow Winter," in his book *The Children's Blizzard*. The storms began early, on October 15, with a three-day blizzard, followed by more blizzards throughout the winter and early spring. Many homesteaders faced the threat of starvation.

The construction of the Northern Pacific Railroad provided the means of escape and survival for Mary and her daughter. It was in 1880, according to family legend, that she found work as a cook for the construction crew as the tracks extended westward. The single detail of her experience that survives in our family lore is her recollection that she used buffalo "chips" for fuel as they crossed the plains. Dried buffalo droppings burned with little smoke and made an efficient cooking fuel on the plains, where wood was scarce. It took just a few minutes to gather the three bushels needed for a good fire. Women forced to cook with them were at first squeamish about handling them, but soon got over their reluctance.

Historical research on the construction of the Northern Pacific Railroad, as well as earlier transcontinental projects, casts some light on what life might have been like for Mary and her daughter. The workers, predominantly young Irish and Scandinavian immigrants, took great pride in the contribution they were making toward the "Manifest Destiny" of their adopted country. The railroad opened up new territories, with free land, and unimaginable possibilities for people such as themselves. The work was backbreaking, and the men were pushed to their limits, but all agreed it was an exciting endeavor. Mary's stories about those exhilarating days must have marked her as an adventurer, and a bit of a "rum 'un," as Evelyn Cameron would describe her.

The NPRR had a reputation as a good employer, providing well for its workers. The daily feeding of a small army of young,

Meetings With Mrs. Collins

hard-working men was vital to keeping the construction moving forward smoothly. The end-of-track construction camp was called a "Hotel-on-Wheels," a row of twenty or more cars, including a carpenter shop, blacksmith shop, and a store for the men—like a little rolling village. The workers were paid from $2.50 to $4.00 per day, depending on their job, and they paid $4.50 a week for their board. There were sleeping cars, a kitchen car, and dining cars where they were fed. They ate at long tables set with metal plates and tableware. Huge platters of food were brought out, especially for the mid-day meal. The food was simple and plentiful: roasted and fried meats, potatoes, hot coffee, soup, diluted condensed milk, and canned fruit, pies, or cakes. Perhaps in the evening an Irish song would ring out from the sleeping cars as the men relaxed, played games, or smoked a bit before turning in.

"Railroad building on the Great Plains" by Alfred Rudolph Waud (1828-1891). From *Harper's Weekly*, July 17, 1875, page 577. Mary Collins left Minnesota with her daughter Rose in 1880, working as a cook for the NPRR construction crew until the train reached Miles City, Montana. *Minnesota Historical Society (MHS Locator #HE6.41 N/p3. Negative #11473.)*

As the tracks were laid westward, ranchers from as far away as Texas drove their longhorn steers north to meet the train. Workers filled the cars and sent them east, as many as thirty-seven cars in a day. It was expected that as the rails approached Miles City, the major Montana cattle center, the hauling would become increasingly lucrative.

The railroad also transported another load—buffalo hides. Buffalo hunters at first collected the buffalo robes in winter when coats were thickest. But in 1870, a new process for making commercial leather from the hides increased demand from eastern and foreign leather factories, and made buffalo hunting a year-round business. When the railroad reached the Dakota/Montana boundary it had arrived at the center of the northern plains buffalo range, and Mary and Rose must therefore have witnessed the last days of these huge buffalo herds.

In 1806, Captain William Clark had encountered large numbers of buffalo when he passed through eastern Montana in July and August. Nowadays, Terry residents proudly point out that, on the night of July 30, the expedition had camped a few miles west of the present-day town of Terry. Clark wrote: "During the whole night the buffalo were prowling about camp, and excited much alarm, lest in crossing the river they should tread on the boats and split them to pieces." Clark's journal reveals the immensity of these herds. On Sunday afternoon, August 1, he reported a "gangue of Buffalow" a mile wide crossing the Yellowstone, forcing the men to pull their boats to shore and wait an hour for the herd to cross.

Whites had already cleared the southern range of buffalo in an extravagantly wasteful manner. Both the Indians and the buffalo were seen by many to be an impediment to America's Manifest Destiny. Sport hunters were urged to "kill every buffalo you can! Every buffalo dead is an Indian gone." Up until the 1870s, buffalo hunters were reluctant to venture into the northern plains, where hostile Indian tribes desperately held on to their lands, their way of life, and their buffalo. That began to change when, in 1872, the NPRR began surveying in the Yellowstone River Valley. One of their survey parties in 1873 was under the protection of the Seventh Cavalry, led by General George Armstrong Custer. After several years of violent encounters with local tribes, Custer met defeat on June 25, 1876, at the Battle of the Little Bighorn.

Colonel Nelson Miles soon redoubled his efforts to force the Indians to surrender. Sitting Bull and his followers continued to assert their right to hunt in the Yellowstone Valley, but after an incident at Coal Creek, south of Terry, they fled to Canada along with the Northern Cheyenne. Chief Crazy Horse later surrendered, and within a few years eastern Montana was deemed safe enough to encourage the buffalo hunters to move into the territory and continue their unimpeded decimation of the buffalo.

Mary and Rose must have seen the buffalo hunters' wagons, heavily loaded with hides, as they lumbered across the prairie to meet the train. They may even have caught sight of a little boat, the *Terry*, piled high with ten thousand buffalo hides as it floated downstream to meet the *C.K. Peck* on the Missouri.

Although track laying had stopped for the winter, grading and rock excavation continued south of the Yellowstone River, with a work crew about 300 strong. By July 22, 1881, regular trains were able to make it into Glendive, setting off a "boom" in that town. Hundreds of buffalo hunters brought their hides to sell and trade. Northern Pacific Railroad cars transported the hides to the eastern U.S., to tanners there and in foreign countries.

West of Glendive, unforeseen difficulties arose, and between early July and mid-September the track laying progressed only 30 miles, due to the clay bluffs repeatedly crumbling into the river.

Mary and Rose must have been fascinated by the cowboys they observed at various points along the Yellowstone River, driving their cattle across the prairie, and loading them onto the railroad cars. They likely witnessed a scene like this one, described in the *Official Northern Pacific Railroad Guide*, published in 1894:

> As the train passes through the Yellowstone valley, it is no uncommon sight to see herds of sleek cattle contentedly grazing on the russet hills. Sometimes, also, droves of one or two thousand are noticed slowly advancing in a broad column from the direction of the distant mountains on their way to the railroad

shipping stations. Such a drove is kept well in hand by a number of herders, picturesquely garbed in sombreros, gray shirts and leather breeches called "chapps," each man being armed with revolver, bowie knife and a rawhide whip, and well mounted. If the drove of cattle has made a march of several hundred miles from the range, it will be pioneered by a large band of ponies, carrying camp equipage and supplies, and serving as remounts for the cow boys. These latter are usually brawny, clear-eyed fellows, civil enough to answer questions in spite of the fact that every fibre of both man and horse seems strained to its utmost tension in keeping the wilder and straying members of the drove within the bounds of the horned column.

The rails finally reached Terry on October 8, 1881, and Miles City the week before Christmas. It was most likely in Miles City, a well-established town that was enjoying a boom from the increased traffic brought by the railroad, that Mary decided to "jump ship" and start a boardinghouse of her own. With its multitudes of Texas cowboys, and American, English, and Scottish cattlemen, as well as buffalo hunters, railroad workers, sheepherders, and soldiers, Miles City initially seemed to offer Mary the new chance in life she was seeking.

The evidence of Mary's presence in Miles City is found in a book titled *This Last West: Miles City, Montana Territory, and Environs, 1876-1886*, by Lorman L. Hoopes, M.D., which includes a directory of early residents of the town. It lists: "Collins, Mary: '82: housekeeper, corner 6 and Pleasant." This location may have been the site of her first boardinghouse in Montana, or perhaps it was a dwelling where she took in boarders to make a living.

Interestingly, other Terry pioneers had also started out in Miles City. Frederick Zahl, known as "Doc" Zahl, was formerly a buffalo hunter in the "Big Open," the vast lands between the Missouri and Yellowstone rivers. He subsequently operated the "Powder River House," hiring a Mrs. Mary Miller as manager—"ample accommodations for man and beast." Mrs. Miller became his wife in 1881, but a year later they divorced. Zahl then married Caroline Batelle. The couple later moved to Terry and opened the Zahl Hotel there. (Frank Stith helped build the hotel in 1884.) "Doc" became the Deputy Sheriff of Terry in 1884.

After her divorce in 1882, the former Mrs. Zahl "use[d] George H. Towne's residence, at 6 and Pleasant, as a boarding house." This would have made her a close neighbor of Mary Collins. Rose Collins is not listed in the Miles City School census.

Joe Laundre, who would later be Mary Collins' neighbor on their homesteads east of Terry, apparently also once lived in Miles City, as his son Henry attended the Miles City School in 1883.

In 1882, Miles City, named for Colonel Nelson A. Miles and sometimes called "Milestown," was a busy commercial hub for cattlemen and cowboys, as well as for the last of the buffalo hunters, who would go "belly-ups" the following year when it became apparent there were no more buffalo to hunt.

One Miles City regular was "Teddy Blue" Abbott, whose memoirs of his wild days and nights in Miles City helped inspire Larry McMurtry's book *Buffalo Girls*. Abbott's friend Martha Canary, alias Calamity Jane, appeared in Miles City on February 11, 1882, and briefly settled on a ranch to the west of town. From there, she made occasional visits to Miles City that summer, most notably on the Fourth of July, when she indulged in a wild night of drunkenness and revelry.

The corner of Sixth and Pleasant, where Mary operated her boardinghouse, was, for better or for worse, located only a block away from the excitement of Main Street. In his book *Recollections of Old Milestown* (1918), Samuel Gordon describes the street as lined with businesses appealing to the male population's coarser appetites and recreations. On one corner of Sixth and Main stood the Cosmopolitan Theater, one of several popular venues for variety shows. On another corner was C. W. Savage & Sons, where summer afternoon "water-fights" were staged weekly using "four-man force pumps." On nice days the street was often cleared for football games and horseracing. A major spectacle was the "Diamond R bull-train" parading down Main on its way to Fort Keogh with its load of government freight. Lining the three blocks of Sixth Street between the theater and the Northern Pacific depot were rows of "Parlor Houses," or brothels. A block to the west

"Bull Train, corner of Main and Park Streets," Miles City, Montana, 1881. In 1882, Mary Collins took in boarders at her home nearby, at Sixth and Pleasant Streets. *L. A. Huffman photograph, courtesy of the Montana Historical Society (981-523).*

down Main was the Charley Brown Saloon, one of many watering holes, famous for its huge pot of free Mulligan stew.

Gordon also describes a darker side of the town: with the railroad's arrival in Miles City came an influx of disreputable toughs, hobos and tramps from the Eastern cities, attracted to the town's free and easy life style. Local citizens were alarmed at the sudden increase in crime, as well as the frequent insults to women. Things came to a head on July 21, 1883, when a local vigilante group lynched a lawbreaker named Rigner. Shortly following the lynching, a suspicious fire broke out in the Cosmopolitan Theater, which burned down nearly the entire block. The lynching was never investigated and the "suspicious characters" quickly left town.

Mary had many reasons to leave Miles City. Fires were a common occurrence, as were floods. There was also concern for Rose's safety, and her future. Women were in short supply, and her daughter was blossoming into a lovely young lady, no doubt attracting some unwanted advances. They could have chosen to join the flood of Irish men and women heading west to the new copper mines of Butte, but forty miles to the east, the little town of Terry was being settled by a gentler breed of newcomer, and business opportunities were opening up, even for a lone woman. Most likely in 1883, Mary made the decision that would launch the next chapter of her life.

* * *

How much of this Mary actually told Evelyn over lunch is, of course, pure conjecture. But it's not hard to imagine that, as Mary relived her past, the two women realized they were revisiting moments in history that had brought great changes to the northern plains. They must have shared the premonition that the era they were a part of would soon come to a close.

After lunch Evelyn did a few chores in town, "To Mrs. G's [Gipson]. Got us beef, collected her old barrels for putting on pie plants, got ham, bacon, matches at McDonald's. Also a granite pot 1.50¢ & a granite pail from Stith, 50¢, very cheap."

When she arrived home at five o'clock, she did her round of chores and prepared supper: "Ham, eggs, fried taters, prunes & apple compote, rice pudding, coffee." In the evening she developed her glass plates, "2 of hanging Alec & one at the plough. I stayed to catch on more at the art." She wrote her diary entry at 10:40 and retired for the night. But soon, her very pregnant cat awakened her:

Colleen Elizabeth Carter

Kindlings kept mewing after me. I finally concluded she was suffering the pains of labour, her tum very enlarged & sore soothingly rubbed seemed to suit her complaint, [leaving] a discharge behind which didn't improve my skirt. Put her in a box with paper and gunny sacks [where] she was content to lie. [Went to] bed 12.00. 12.20—Since writing, Kindle has given birth to a kitten. She purrs loud & continuously the whole time.

* * *

"From the flowerlike snow peaks of Oregon to the waterless red lands of Arizona dwells a spirit that, once it has touched the wanderer, leaves him homeless in all other places for ever after.' 'The Spell of the West' From 'The Sun' Nov. 4th '06"
—Written inside the front cover of Evelyn's 1906 diary.

Chapter 11

"I saw the dead wee thing laid out with white flowers on its little white coffin."

TUESDAY, JULY 23, 1895
Dug 140# tatoes. To Terry in wagon. Developed. Bed 2.45.
Glorious. Thunder storm threatened evening. Passes away.

Evelyn arose at six forty-five. She was grateful for Alec's help as they harvested vegetables to sell in Terry that afternoon. "Alec got up also at that hour & grubbed up tatoes kindly for me but it is slow work in hot sun for such quantities to be unearthed." After serving breakfast at nine thirty, she washed up and went "down to garden & dug while Alec picked up the potatoes. It took til 1.40. I helped Alec make bunches of young carrots & onions. Quite a market show. Altogether sacked up 100#, 10#, 60# at 3¢ per lb. Not bad." Ewen enjoyed a much less strenuous morning, writing letters.

After lunch at two fifteen, Evelyn dressed while Ewen readied the wagon team. The three headed down to Terry, their wagon loaded with produce. At the post office Evelyn sent off a letter and a "$12.50 order to the Detroit Allen (photographer)"—an order for photographic supplies. She bought "glass & cutter to put in printing frames" at Stith's.

Then she "went to call at Mrs. Collins." There she came upon a grim scene: "her daughter Rosie Ingersol staying with her, lost her 6 month old little girl last night. Ill 24 hours. Supposed to have been cholera "inflatum" or some such name. They were very cut up. I saw the dead wee thing laid out with white flowers on its little white coffin. [Half] closed eyes, pink colour in its cheeks."

Evelyn's diary does not say to whom she sold her produce that day—presumably some of it had been intended for Mrs. Collins. (Three days later she would sell Mary twenty-five pounds of potatoes, "1¢ pr #.") After buying eighteen pounds of meat from Mrs. Jordan she picked up the glasscutter and a winch and headed home.

Although she did not serve supper until nine o'clock that evening, Evelyn's long day was far from over—she worked five and a half more hours, developing film late into the night, finally getting to bed at two forty-five a.m. By that time, pure exhaustion made her put off writing in her diary until the next evening.

* * *

Evelyn most likely had met Mary's daughter Rosie, and her husband, who was a prominent Miles City rancher. Rose Collins had left Terry some time in the late 1880s to teach school in Miles City. Our family lore claims that she taught school at the age of fourteen, when she and her mother first arrived in Montana, but I have not been able to confirm this. School census records for 1885 and 1886 show her as a student in Terry at age eighteen and nineteen. This may indicate that she was not a teacher until at least 1887, by which time she would have been twenty.

The one photograph we have of Rose shows a mature woman with soft, lovely features and the hint of a smile, her beautiful dark eyes gazing confidently at the camera. Having inherited much of her mother's drive and ambition, she was in no great hurry to marry. Her mother had lived a life of suffering and hard work, and

Meetings With Mrs. Collins

Unidentified infant in casket. When Mary Collins' granddaughter Ruth died of infant cholera in 1895, Evelyn wrote: "I saw the dead wee thing laid out with white flowers on its little white coffin." *Cameron photograph, courtesy of the Prairie County Museum, Terry, Montana. (Box IX, Neg. 7, EC43)*

would have wanted something better for her daughter. In Irish society, a teacher was regarded with the utmost esteem, and in America, teaching was one of the few respectable professions open to women. On the frontier, some started as young as fifteen, no teaching certificate being required. While teaching school in Miles City, Rose set her sights on a handsome, eligible bachelor, eight years her senior, George F. Ingersoll. A colorful account of his life was written by their son Lynn and given to Mary Haughian, the Prairie County Museum volunteer who now owns his ranch:

> G. F. Ingersoll originally from Lynn, Mass., and Boone Iowa, after graduating from Mount Vernon, Iowa college decided to "Go West Young Man Go West" as the famous editor of the New York Times Newspaper Horace Greely, said. After a trip

all over the Western U.S. he headed for the Black Hills Gold Rush 1875, but wound up at Old Tascosa on the North Canadian river, not far North of where Amarillo, Tex—quite a city now, stands.

After punching cows and keeping books—so on and so forth and he got to be trail boss or foreman of two herds of 3000 steers each headed for the big grass country of Eastern Mont., between the Yellowstone and Big Missouri Rivers. These herds of young steers were from the Lee-Scott (LS) out fit on the North Canadian River range and were being sent up North to develope into 5 & 6 yr. old steers weighing on an average of 1200 lbs in Chicago Ill. which was a direct market from Mont. on the Northern Pacific R.R.—first across Mont., year of 1882. These two LS herds landed on the Big Dry at the mouth of what is still called LS Creek, 20 miles below what is now the town of Jordan in later day Garfield Co.

The book *Wheels Across Montana's Prairie*, compiled by the Prairie County Historical Society, contains a biography written by Ingersoll's daughter Dixie for the Range Riders Museum in Miles City. In it she states that on June 25, 1890, George Ingersoll married Rose Collins, a teacher in the Miles City school. They had three children, Lynn, Dixie, and Dick.

* * *

What Evelyn described as cholera "inflatum" was undoubtedly *cholera infantum,* or infant cholera. In her diary she remarked that the baby had been sick only 24 hours. This was a noted symptom of the illness. In a short period of time, a healthy child could suffer severe vomiting and intestinal spasms and then collapse into death. The disease struck fear in the hearts of helpless parents.

The death of Mary's granddaughter, named Ruth, cast a dark shadow over the family for many years to come. Lynn Ingersoll, only six years old when his sister died, would, in his old age, still mourn her death, as well as the death of a brother named John. He even took Mary Haughian on a futile search for their graves in

Mary Collins' daughter, Rose (1866-1945). She accompanied her mother to Montana in 1880, at the age of fourteen, later taught school in Miles City, then married prominent cattle rancher George F. Ingersoll. *Collection of author.*

Miles City, telling her they had died of "summer complaints–bad milk." This illness, called *Morbo Laocteo*, which may have killed baby John, was a medical mystery until the 1920s. Affecting cattle and humans alike, the agonizingly painful disease was finally traced to poisonous plants.

It is not hard to imagine the helpless desperation Mary and Rose felt as they were forced to watch little Ruth's suffering. The fact that children died frequently in those days did not make the family's grief less wrenching, and they mourned with the intensity of love bestowed on one dying so young. It would have been no surprise if both mother and grandmother suffered nervous debilities in the aftermath.

* * *

TUESDAY, SEPTEMBER 24, 1895
<u>Ewen & I in wagon to Terry afternoon. Home about 7.</u>
Equanoctial weather, dull & windy.

Evelyn arose at six thirty, milked the cows, and served breakfast at nine o'clock. After cleaning up, she made jam and jelly from black currants picked the day before. She and Ewen left for Terry at about three fifteen. They stopped first at the post office to console Mrs. Furnish, whose mother had just died in a tragic accident: "It was 73 feet she fell down elevator instant death no witness 'cept porter boy whose evidence is worthless because probably happened thro' his carelessness."

They next visited Mrs. Collins—it would be the last they would see of her for a while. "Bought from Mrs. Collins 1 mattress $2, 1 single springs $3, 1 chamber [pot?] $1, 1 pillow $1. She is going next month to Minn. for 1 year."

When the Camerons returned home from their trip to Terry it was dark. Evelyn warmed up roast chicken from the night before. Evelyn had remarked in her diary, "Blowflies got into chickens had to wash them out, then stuffed with onion & oatmeal liver & gizz..."

Meetings With Mrs. Collins

* * *

In Jackson, Minnesota lived Maude Auten, Mary's oldest daughter, who may have suggested the visit as a way of helping her mother recover from the recent loss. The train would pass through Fargo, making it likely that she stopped to visit her son James in nearby Page, North Dakota. This would have provided an opportunity to see her six-year-old grandson William.

During Mary's absence, the Laundre family occupied her house for a time. Evelyn and Ewen visited them there on May 17, 1896: "Mrs. Laundre is in Mrs. Collins' house she is dying of consumption her husband & children are with her." Evelyn saw Mrs. Laundre again on June 4: "She looks awfully ill. Poor Laundre lay on a couch at the foot of her bed (she cannot bear him out of her sight.) Her laboured weary breathing sounds bad. Stopt only a few minutes she was unable to talk."

* * *

The months during Mrs. Collins' absence brought no relief to the Cameron's financial struggles. According to Donna Lucey, the year 1895 had begun with great expectations. Ewen had entered into a business venture with a wealthy man in Scotland, T. B. Dryborough, a polo player, who wished to import Montana horses and sell them as polo ponies. But, from the beginning, the enterprise was plagued with problems, and they had not made any profit from their efforts so far.

It was actually Evelyn who did most of the work of breaking in the horses. In spite of this additional work, Evelyn continued to devote herself to mastering photographic techniques, under the guidance of Mr. Colley. In June 1895, she had purchased a new No. 5 Kodet camera, in which she could use either 5" x 7" glass plates or sheets of film. In August, on a weeklong stay in Miles City, Evelyn purchased a photograph from L. A. Huffman, a pioneer photographer. He became an inspiration to her in her quest to develop her skills to a professional level.

Mr. Colley left at the end of 1895. His departure left Ewen and

Evelyn disappointed that neither of their "impecunious boarders" had chosen to invest money in their ranch as they had hoped, but for Evelyn it was a relief that now there would now be one less man in the house to make demands on her.

In August 1896, the Camerons enjoyed several weeks visiting friends at the Cross S Ranch during the fall horse races in Miles City. If Evelyn's trips to Terry were few and far between, her opportunities to visit her British compatriots near Miles City were even more rare. Though infrequent, these trips were important for both social and business reasons. When they stayed at the Macqueen House, a popular gathering place for British cattlemen, or while visiting the ranches of friends, Evelyn occasionally was obliged to borrow clothing in order to be appropriately attired.

That fall they returned to the Cross S Ranch to help their soon-to-be-wed friend Walter Lindsay, an aristocratic Anglo-Irishman, build and decorate new rooms. There, Evelyn would befriend a cultured young American governess, Fannie McElrath, daughter of one of Miles City's founders and granddaughter of a former publishing partner of Horace Greely.

* * *

Mrs. Collins returned to Terry in the fall of 1896. On November 21, Evelyn paid her a visit, attired in her "Scott Adie Ulster" skirt: "I went to see Mrs. Collins (who had shrieked for me to go & see her) She gave me a very fine rich plum cake [with a] little suet in it." The word "shrieked" carries a hint of annoyance. Indeed, for the next six months, Evelyn makes no mention of Mrs. Collins in her diary.

In May 1897, Evelyn's diary would contain a curious remark—a clue to their apparent estrangement.

* * *

Meetings With Mrs. Collins

"The Tragedy" by Charles Edwin Markham
   "Oh, the fret of the brain,
And the wounds & the worry;
Oh, the thought of love & the thought of death—
And the soul in its silent hurry.
      But the stars break above,
      And the fields flower under;
      And the tragical life of man goes on,
      Surrounded by beauty & wonder."

—Written inside the back cover of Evelyn's 1898 diary.

Chapter 12

*"Mrs. Collins never drank now...
unless she got into the blues."*

WEDNESDAY, MAY 19, 1897
<u>Ewen & I drove to Terry. Got pair boots, etc. Home 7.</u>
Lovely. Cool wind.

Evelyn arose at seven o'clock to a pleasantly warm morning. During her round of chores, she found two new chicks in the hen house. Later in the morning, Ewen readied the wagon team. They set off for Terry at about twelve fifteen. Alec had sent along some of his bundles of "pie plant," or rhubarb, which Evelyn sold at ten cents per bundle to Mrs. Scott, Mrs. Gipson, and Mrs. Stith. Their purchases in town included: "5 yards of oil cloth, 2¢ per yard at Gipson's, cream of tarter, 6 oz., 25¢, 1 lb. ginger, 35¢, 1 pr. 5 1/2 boys lace up boots, $2.00. Got 50 lb. lime from Stith, an 80¢ milk pail earthenware bowl, 90¢ fruit glass bowl. Got 2 W.C. boxes from Hamlin."

Evelyn stopped at the post office, now in the log-cabin home of

Susie Snow, to loan Mr. Snow a copy of "Banners," *The Banner of Israel* magazine, a publication of the Imperial British-Israel Association, which Donna Lucey describes as "a group that believed the inhabitants of Britain and its scattered Empire were actually the ten lost tribes of Israel." Evelyn had recently begun a personal campaign to interest some of Terry's residents in the organization's apocalyptic interpretations of world affairs—a strange project for someone so commonsensical in her daily life, and not something likely to excite Americans, but which she took on with her usual enthusiasm. In a letter to Ewen's mother of March 7, 1896, she had written, "I have 'sown some British Israel seed' in Terry where I hope it will germinate, but the people there are not very ambitious for enlightenment beyond their St. Paul or Chicago weekly."

Leaving Terry for home, they stopped briefly to visit neighbors, and at seven o'clock arrived at the ranch. Evelyn was "rather annoyed" that Alec had lit a fire, probably in anticipation of a hot supper. Her plans for the evening, however, did not include cooking: "Had cold supper."

Writing in her diary that night, almost as an afterthought, Evelyn added this comment: "Mrs. Gipson assured me that Mrs. Collins never drank now, in fact never unless she got into the blues & she thought she would suit us well."

* * *

"Mrs. Collins never drank now . . ." Maybe it was her granddaughter's death; maybe that loss brought back the despair of losing her beloved daughter Sarah in 1872; maybe the ghosts of the Irish Potato Famine had risen to haunt her. But the result was a bad case of "the blues." On the frontier it was not uncommon for women to turn to the bottle for consolation and for "medicinal purposes," as a cure for depression or a nervous condition. Many became alcoholics as a result. There is an anecdote in our family lore about the young Elizabeth Preston, a close friend of my great-grandmother Lilla Pannebaker (whose granddaughter would wed Mary Collins' grandson William Collins in 1912). The two young women, left alone one night at the Pannebaker's Dakota tree claim, became frightened by noises outside the cabin. What they feared were Indians turned out to be the oxen, which, having gotten loose, were milling around outside. Recovering from the shock, Miss Preston inquired, "Mrs. Pannebaker, does Mr. Pannebaker have a little whisky in the house—just for 'medicinal purposes?'" And Lilla said, "Yes, he has some—for 'medicinal purposes.'" To which Miss Preston rejoined, "Let's have some!"

Ironically, Miss Preston would later become a Prohibitionist and North Dakota leader of the Women's Christian Temperance Union. She had firsthand knowledge of the dangers of alcohol. Having a fragile constitution, she suffered a nervous breakdown due to the hardships of her early pioneering years. She described her experience with alcohol in her autobiography, *Under the Prairie Winds:*

> My physician prescribed alcoholic liquor as a stimulant. In those days, even doctors did not recognize alcohol as a narcotic. After several weeks, I found myself watching the clock in my desire for the next dose of medicine. I did not know then that alcohol was a habit-forming drug . . . However, a few weeks of the "medication" awakened me to what I might expect if it were continued. I immediately stopped taking it, and when I told the doctor why, he laughed uproariously. It was a joke to him, but I had learned a great lesson.

Being Irish made Mary especially vulnerable to alcoholism. In fact, many Irish immigrant women, due to their earlier sufferings, were at times emotionally unstable and quite prone to the "curse of intemperance." Many Irish Catholic women did abstain from alcohol, but Mary was not among them. Her daughter Rose would remember her lifelong love of beer, and that she always kept a supply on hand in her basement. Given Mary's means of making a living, the townsfolk of Terry must have seen her often in a state of intoxication during her "blue" periods. There were many upstanding citizens in town, particularly the Protestant women, who would have disapproved—who saw drunkenness as a private sin, to be hidden in the confines of one's home.

Wherever "the blues" led Mary during this time of tribulation, it seems to have put a temporary end to Evelyn's visits. Evelyn, who suffered her losses with a typically British "stiff upper lip," likely viewed Mary's behavior as weak-minded. To her, there were no emotional difficulties that could not be relieved by long walks and hard physical work. As she would write to a friend in December 1897: "These are the tonics that will make you feel the world is not such a bad place after all . . ."

Six months after her last visit with Mary, Evelyn inquired delicately after her old friend and got the news that the drinking, for the most part, had ceased. The phrase "she thought she would suit us well," suggests that Evelyn and Ewen had some favor to ask of Mary.

One thing we know about this period in Mary's life, thanks to old property records, is that four months earlier, on January 21, 1897, she had sold her homestead to George T. Gipson, the husband of the woman whom Evelyn questioned about Mrs. Collins' condition. Gipson, a former cowboy from Texas, ran a general store in Terry. It's possible that Mary sold the property because it had become a burden to her. But county records show that even more real estate deals were to follow, indicating that the homestead had probably been acquired with a view to speculation.

* * *

WEDNESDAY, JUNE 16, 1897
<u>Scrubbed kitchen. Down to Terry with wagon. Got back late. Mrs. Collins will not come to cook.</u>
Morn bright. Clouded up. Poured 3 pm.

Evelyn arose at 5:10. After breakfast, the Camerons went to the corral to look at a new bunch of unbroken ponies. They caught, blindfolded, and measured a black "oss," and were disappointed to find that it "turned out to be only 152 [centimeters] not higher than Buttermilk. So Ewen had him turned out again as useless there are only 3 or 4 out of the 11 that are any good at all [the rest] are too small."

After a "cold lunch" at twelve thirty, Evelyn "put sheets on our bed today for 1st time." They left for Terry at two thirty, and were delayed by a sudden afternoon rainstorm: "Just before getting to Landre's house it began to rain & kept it up with a tremendous downpour. Ewen took team out & put them in Hamlin's barn. Hamlin just got going up to Miles (great swell) as witness for Charlie Prior. Many others going also. I stayed at the Hamlins till 5. Then got in wagon again."

When she wrote in her diary that night, Evelyn made no mention of a visit to Mrs. Collins, but at the top of the page she noted: "Mrs. Collins will not come to cook." This, of course, is what Evelyn had had in mind when she asked Mrs. Gipson about Mary's drinking.

The diary entries for the previous month show a flurry of cleaning, painting, and decorating, all in anticipation of a visit from their Miles City friends, Walter Lindsay and his new wife. Alec's bedroom was transformed to receive the couple: "Put cheese cloth up on Alec's ceiling, puttied cracks, stained, oiled floor." The walls were "blue washed," and "Alec painted around doors & windows." New curtains, made by Mrs. Hamlin, were installed. The kitchen was cleaned and the walls "yellow washed."

Evelyn had hoped to find a cook, thus leaving herself free to enjoy her guests, but she had not been able to persuade Mrs. Collins to help. Perhaps Mary was not inclined to act as servant to the Cameron's aristocratic Anglo-Irish friends. The next day, Evelyn went to find a Mrs. Olynger, who also declined, saying that she had to cook for "5 men who were going to paint the RR bridge at Powder River."

The Lindsays arrived the evening of June 20, and Alec set up a tent outside to sleep in. Evelyn had found a cook, a Mrs. Anderson, who had done some sewing for her. The next morning, however, while Evelyn helped her prepare breakfast, Mrs. Anderson suddenly became ill with severe "indigestion pains." Evelyn's morning was taken up with preparing baths, chopping wood, and carrying coal, all the while trying to entertain her guests.

The English custom of afternoon tea was not a part of the normal Eve Ranch routine, but Evelyn knew the Lindsays would expect it. A simple one, "buns [and] buttered toast," was served at

5:20. Mrs. Anderson was still ill, so Evelyn cooked supper alone. At seven fifteen she served "Eng[lish] hash, minced poached eggs, fried tato, salad, pie cold, fruit." Mrs. Anderson had "toast, lemonade, mince egg."

For breakfast the next morning Evelyn made "self raising buckwheat pancakes." Mrs. Anderson was "better but weak & unable to work," so Alec accompanied her back to Terry. Evelyn served dinner at one thirty: "Irish stew, bak. batter [dumplings?] nectarines."

As Evelyn began feeling overwhelmed, she thought of young Mabel Joubert. She dashed off on the horse Sunflower, now fitted with an English saddle, and soon arrived at the Joubert ranch near Terry. Over a glass of chokecherry wine, she asked Mabel if she would come to Eve Ranch to cook. Mable agreed—if Evelyn could get her mother's consent. Evelyn found Mabel's mother at the Terry Hotel, visiting the Braleys. Mrs. Joubert was reluctant to let her daughter go, saying they had twelve to cook for, but finally relented. Evelyn found Alec and asked him to get Mabel and bring her to the ranch on "Jumbo."

Thus was Evelyn able to relax a bit and enjoy the remainder of the Lindsay's visit. The couple left by train on the twenty-fifth. The next evening, Evelyn wrote at the top of her diary page: "Every visitor's gone . . . sorry they have gone yet nice to be quiet."

* * *

"We started from Southhampton to-day 6 years ago."
—Evelyn Cameron's diary, September 13, 1897

Chapter 13

"She says she will go to Klondike with me & we are to keep an hotel."

MONDAY, OCTOBER 25, 1897
Rode to Terry. Paid Stith. Called on Mrs. Arnold & Mrs. Collins.
Dull. Rained from 7 to 10. Cleared. Wind got up 12:30.

Evelyn arose at seven fifteen and put breakfast on to cook while she went out to milk the cows. At eight thirty, she served a breakfast of "mince, fried tato." She washed up and swept, then saddled her horse Pilot for the trip to town. "Alec wanted to go but I told him it was quite useless for us both to go. I went alone. Rode down thro Landres pasture."

With great anticipation Evelyn called for her mail at the post office, and she was relieved to find two letters from Ewen. It was nearly three months since she had seen him. The previous summer, Ewen had insisted that he himself would accompany the next shipment of fifteen horses to Mr. Drybrough in England.

On July 29, while loading the horses at Fallon, the horse he

93

was riding fell, and Ewen suffered a serious blow to the head. Evelyn wrote:

> I found him being supported along by George Rock. We got him in the caboose he could walk & talk but knew not where or for what purpose he had come. Vomited often. Cogshall, Kempton, trainmen, cowboys came in to look at Ewen. I took Ewen to Terry 3.20 train . . . Went to Scott's [Hotel] questions filled the air. Nice 2 windowed rm upstairs. Got him to bed. Supp I had. Ewen drank down some broth. His head splitting. Kept ice on it & he sucked ice. 2 drops of camphor in water to keep down the vomit.

By August 9, he had recovered enough to leave for England. Evelyn accompanied him to the station, taking her clock along "to get the right time." She described him looking like a "great swell" with his "yellow duck waistcoat, new shepherd's check trousers, new tie & Lindsay pink shirt. Best old coat, cap." In a letter to her sister-in-law Jessie Cameron, Evelyn wrote: "I never felt so lonely in my life as I did for some days after his departure."

The trip was a disaster. In the course of Ewen's voyage, two horses died. Shortly after landing, some of the remaining horses began dying of pneumonia, and by early October six horses had died. Ewen and Drybrough held the steamship company accountable, and became embroiled in a fight to get insurance payments plus damages. To make matters worse, Drybrough was not pleased with the surviving horses, finding them too wild and excitable to make civilized polo ponies.

One of the letters Evelyn received from Ewen contained wonderful news—he planned to head for home the second week in November.

Evelyn went to Stith's and paid a bill in the amount of $37.81. She was annoyed when John Stith mentioned a loan that Alec wanted to make to someone, saying, "that he could do so safely with a mortgage on his cattle etc." Evelyn and Ewen were exasperated by some of Alec's irresponsible financial dealings. On April 5, 1893, shortly after he had come to live with them, they "had

Meetings With Mrs. Collins

business talk with Alec . . . I gave it him all round, improvidence, lack of ambition, Etc. Etc." As she wrote in her diary: "I very cross with Alec. Ewen wants Alec to have his quarterly paid to Ewen's account in London."

Evelyn went to see a Mrs. Arnold, who had expressed interest in having her boy "taken" (photographed). Evelyn was finally beginning to realize some financial gain from all her hard work, and much of her early photographic business was in the town of Terry. Mrs. Arnold "said she would let me know in a little while. Her sister [was] there also. We chatted. They dislike Terry very much."

Having gotten all of her business out of the way, Evelyn visited Mrs. Collins. "[We] had good beef steak & bread, green tea. Was hungry." The town was abuzz with talk of gold in the Klondike, and Evelyn discovered that Mrs. Collins, too, had "gold fever." On July 3, "Old Snow," the postmaster, had "gone to the river to try the sand [for] prospects of gold." Evelyn had seen him later that day: "Saw Snow returned from panning out he had a little gold in his sand only stayed 1/2 hour about going to try again."

The town of Terry had once experienced its own brief moment of gold fever, which had come to naught. On May 25, 1884, John Stith wrote his fiancé: "There is a great excitement over a gold mine that was found day before yesterday about 35 miles from here they have layed out a town all ready there was a party of prospecters left her to go out their this morning if it turns out good that will give me all I can do at my trade, for years, and that is as good as a gold mine to me property will be booming."

* * *

The first Klondike gold strike occurred on August 17, 1896, near Dawson, and the local settlers were the first to stake their claims that fall. The next summer these fortunate ones—both men and women—bags heavy with gold, loaded their wealth on steamships and headed for Seattle and San Francisco. Word of the gold discovery spread like wildfire and it was not long before every available vessel was filled with gold-seekers heading to the Klondike.

Soon, however, the newspapers were full of dire warnings. Many of the "stampeders" had left in such a rush that they had not adequately prepared for what lay ahead. Those who turned back, defeated, told harrowing stories of scarce supplies and harsh conditions. Newspaper headlines warned that conditions in the Klondike were too dangerous and arduous for women. Nonetheless, many did follow the lure of gold and adventure, even many lone women, including small-business entrepreneurs, doctors, teachers, nuns, entertainers, and journalists.

On August 5, 1897, Evelyn had written in her diary: "Everybody in Terry wants to sell out & go to the Yukon River in Alaska where this extraordinary find of gold is." The train depot must have drawn curious townsfolk anxious to get a look at the stampeders as they headed west to the Northern Pacific Railroad terminus in Tacoma, Washington, a major port from which many steamships were leaving that summer. Mary Collins, with extra cash from the sale of her homestead to Mr. Gipson that January, was among those tempted to take off for the gold fields, but at her age a partner would be helpful—and who better than the hardy, adventurous Mrs. Cameron?

That night, Evelyn wrote at the top of her diary page: "She [Mrs. Collins] says she will go to Klondike with me & we are to keep an hotel."

Even if Evelyn had agreed to such a rash plan, it was very fortunate that Mary did not heed her impulse to join the stampede. It was already too late to make it to the Klondike before winter set in. On September 13, Evelyn had written in her diary, "Many people will have to starve to death up in the Klondike region owing to scarcity of provisions & it is getting too late for ships to bring them back."

By July of the next summer the gold rush was over.

* * *

"He who striveth for the mastery is temperate in all things."
   —Written on the title page of Evelyn's 1897 diary.

Chapter 14

"She is a dear old body, I think."

FRIDAY, DECEMBER 31, 1897
I rode Pilot to Terry. Visited Bright, Atterburg, Collins, Hamlin & Scotts.
Perfect day. Very bright, calm, clear.

Evelyn arose at seven thirty, observing that the temperature was one degree below zero. She put breakfast on to cook and went out to milk the cows, returning to eat at nine o'clock. Later she washed up, fed the chicks, watered her horse Pilot, fed the cats, and "worked up sponge" for bread.

Letter writing occupied the rest of the morning. She picked up the letter she had written to Ewen the night before—she would add a P.S. before taking it to the post office. He had not left England in November after all, and she and Alec had just spent Christmas without him, so strapped for money they could not afford the traditional goose.

Evelyn also wrote to Fanny McElrath, the young woman she had met at the Cross S Ranch, responding to a recent letter in which the young woman had confessed to feeling "so out-of-sorts with the world," and that Evelyn's "strong gentleness seems the spirit of rest. That is God's sweetest gift, is it not—a heart naturally and truly broad and loving & at peace." In closing, Fanny had written, "Forgive me for writing you a little love letter but I feel it very sincerely."

Moved by the young woman's words, and despite her own exhaustion from running the ranch nearly single-handed, Evelyn invited Fanny to visit Eve Ranch. She even suggested that Miss McElrath bring her nephews, the Avery boys, who were in her charge, even though she had confided in her diary, "Do not want them they are so mischievous." Evelyn recorded an excerpt from Miss McElrath's letter, and her reply, in the back of her diary:

My dear Miss McElrath,

Come & stay with me & bring the nephews. Of course you have completely run yourself down by overwork. Change of scene, rest & quiet are the only remedies. At this time of the year I have so many stock chores to do that I do not feel in a position to entertain a guest – but I know you won't mind that & you can help me pitch hay, feed chickens etc.!

These are the tonics that will make you feel the world is not such a bad place after all . . .

With much love – best wishes for the New Year & hoping to see you soon. Believe me dear Miss McElrath, yours affectionately.
Evelyn J. Cameron

Perhaps Fanny, reading between the lines, realized that her friend's kind invitation might not be her own idea of rest, especially with the Avery boys along. When she wrote back declining the offer, Evelyn would reply: "Dear Miss McElrath I am afraid your nerves are overstrung & if I was with you I should insist on you going for a 3 or 4 mile walk with me every day . . ."

At twelve fifteen, Evelyn set off for Terry, riding Pilot. An hour later she arrived at the Terry post office. Waiting for her was a Christmas card from Ewen with a "woman on a grey horse jump-

Meetings With Mrs. Collins

ing post & rails."

She made several calls that afternoon, both business and social. "Mrs. Bright liked the proofs of her baby. Ordered 12! [The large order must have amused Evelyn, because on December 6, she had written, "Over to Bright's, her little (2 or 3 month) baby is the ugliest little creature ever saw."] Mrs. Furnish to arrive today. I called on Mrs. Atterburg, very nice woman. Wiped up for her. We went to look at Avery's 2 puppies. I want one. After a chat I went to Hamlins. [Mr. Hamlin had helped them set up their winter hunting camp on the 1894-95 hunt.] Had lunch there with them. Looked at 5$ sleigh he wants to sell. I said I would think it over for breaking foals to. Can use team in it also."

About her visit to Mrs. Collins she wrote: "She was ill with cold in the chest which she called 'the grip.' We chatted. I made her bed for her. She gave me 1/2 a plum cake I was to take home. She is a dear old body, I think."

It was getting dark, the temperature quickly plummeting from its midday high of eighteen degrees. She stopped in at the Scotts "just to see them a minute." The town was planning its New Year's Eve ball, but Evelyn was anxious to get back to the ranch. She checked the mail again, finding only the *Chicago Record*—no letter from Ewen.

Before leaving town, Evelyn ordered a delivery of five pounds of beef to Mrs. Collins as a New Year's present.

* * *

Evelyn reported two more encounters with Mrs. Collins in 1897:

September 13: "Gathered plums for Mrs. Collins."

November 21: "Tied up at Scott's Mrs. Collins in there. We chatted."

* * *

Colleen Elizabeth Carter

SATURDAY, JANUARY 1, 1898
Printed & toned all day. Chicken on for Mrs. Collins.
7:50 am 3°a [above] 1:10 20°a 2 pm 22°a 6:45 pm 18°a Bed 12:30
Rather dull. Sun shone thro' light clouds.

    The next morning, Evelyn arose at 7:50 and began her chores. She and Alec breakfasted at nine o'clock on "mutton chops, fried tatoes." She wiped up, fed the chickens, hurried through her housework, and started making photographic prints. The work took until 3:40 p.m. In the midst of it, she "put a chicken on boil for broth for Mrs. Collins put some carrots & onions in the pot also."
    At the same time, she put some chickens in the oven to roast, so as to free up the oven for baking bread that evening. At four o'clock, she started her evening chores, feeding their growing menagerie of cows, horses, and chickens. "I found one of 6 youngest chickens dead. Alec didn't feed them last night when I went to Terry." She also noted: "Sciatica is rather painful tonight." After a supper of "roast chicken, tatoes, cabbage, hot plum pudding, Xmas one," she "sat up in the kitchen until 12.30 burnishing and mounting prints, putting them up in packages for posting."

* * *

SUNDAY, JANUARY 2, 1898
Packed up some photos, pasted cuttings [in] diary '97. Read. Alec rode to Terry.
8 am 23°a 12 – 34°a 5:45 pm 26°a
Lovely. Mild Bright. Cloudy rather after[noon].

    Evelyn arose at eight o'clock, milked the cows, and served breakfast at nine thirty. She fed the chickens, swept the house, and washed up. She then readied six packages of photos, using twenty cents worth of stamps. Alec rode off to Terry with the packages, a letter, and "the broth for Mrs. Collins, [a] quavery jelly."
    Evelyn tried to churn butter in the afternoon, a chore that she called "disheartening work," but found that some of the cream was frozen. This gave her an excuse to read until chore time. For dinner

Meetings With Mrs. Collins

there was "cold chicken, pickles, red cabbage & picalili, plum pudding, Etc." She noted in her diary: "Got a nasty cold in throat caught from Mrs. Collins or Mrs. Hamlin. Red plum ginger beer made me sleepy. Bed 10.30"

* * *

SUNDAY, JANUARY 8, 1898
<u>Waggon to Kempton's, Terry. Got 6 lengths flooring.</u>
Glorious day. Mild. Westerly breeze. Bright.

Evelyn arose at 6:40, milked the cows, and cooked up some homemade sausages for breakfast, a special treat for Alec: "He said the sausages were very good." She fed the chicks, then harnessed up the team for the trip to Terry.

She and Alec stopped at the Kemptons on the way. They saw Mary Kempton, and Sarah, who was "washing, her head invisible." Mr. Kempton held forth on the subject of the badlands, "the formation of which he attributes to burning coal banks & the bad water in them from the water coming thro' the burnt ash below the surface. He explains the good water here as the result of there having never been subterranean fires. This theory seems reasonable."

They arrived in Terry at about two in the afternoon. Evelyn took Mrs. Bright "a packet of hair pins, pinched ones," and, with Mrs. Braley, she discussed her problems churning butter. She also saw Mrs. Collins: "She enjoyed the broth but seems very weak tho up & out." On the twenty-second, Evelyn would report that Mary was "much better," however she herself would suffer recurring colds all winter long—perhaps the responsibilities of caring for the ranch in Ewen's absence were wearing her down.

Evelyn and Alec saw "lovely Mabel" at Scotts. They picked up "lumber from wool press platform," and got the mail. Evelyn was relieved to get a long letter from Ewen, with "European news," and newspaper clippings.

On Saturday, February 15, Ewen finally returned. Evelyn had "tea, venison, bread & butter with Mrs. Collins," while waiting for his train. "Mrs. Collins gave me a great deal of Mabel Joubert Jordan Etc. scandal." (Regrettably, Evelyn did not mention any details of the scandal in her diary.)

Ewen was the last to get off when the train arrived. "Oh so glad to see him. We went to Scotts they were arrayed in their very best & had a fire in the parlor. He gave them their Austrian blanket."

Ewen returned home discouraged with his failed horse-raising scheme, but already had plans for a new venture—cattle ranching.

* * *

"Verse on Jessie's Xmas card sent to me Xmas 1897
*   I would flood your path with sunshine,*
I would fence you from all ill,
I would crown you with all blessings,
If I could but have my will!
Ah! but human love may err, dear,
And a power all wise is near,
So I only pray God bless you,
*   and*
God keep you through the year!"
—Written inside back cover of Evelyn's 1897 diary.

Chapter 15

"She has got rail road men boarding with her at $3.75 a week."

TUESDAY, MAY 24, 1898
<u>Mopped rooms. Ewen & I drove our wagon to Terry.</u>
Cloudy & evening wet. North wind.

Evelyn arose at 6:40, milked the cows, fed the chickens, and had breakfast at eight forty-five. After washing up, she mopped the floors in the kitchen and in the main room that served as both bedroom and sitting room. "Keeping the ranch house clean was a never-ending struggle," states Donna Lucey. "On [one] occasion, following a recommendation by her friend Mrs. Collins, she washed the floors with whey. To add a high polish she rubbed them with bacon fat."

Around noon, Evelyn harnessed the wagon team and dressed for the trip to Terry, putting on her "Olan costume, red tam." She and Ewen tied up the dogs and left for Terry at twelve thirty. At Gipson's store, they purchased: "100# shorts [grain for livestock],

7# bacon, 10# tapioca." At Scott's they delivered Alec's rhubarb and "chatted." Evelyn remarked that they had a "very big wash hanging out."

They stopped for a short visit with Mrs. Collins. Evelyn later reported in her diary that Mary had "railroad men boarding with her at $3.75 a week." Evelyn seems to have admired Mrs. Collins' business and real estate dealings. On May 7, 1894, she had noted in her diary: "Spoke to Mrs. Collins in her mansion." She was also interested in the amount of money Mary was able to demand for board and room, especially as she herself had experimented with taking in boarders.

With wages averaging between thirty and forty dollars a month, $3.75 per week represented a considerable chunk of a man's earnings. Many young, unmarried cowboys, ranchers, and railroad workers willingly paid the price to have a "home away from home," where they could count on an ample, well-cooked meal at the end of the day's work. Some men, however, begrudged the weekly payment—in fact, Mary's friend John Stith, in his capacity as Justice of the Peace, occasionally had to arrest cowboys for not paying their boardinghouse bills.

If Mrs. Collins had a bank account, it was probably in Miles City—Terry would not have a bank until 1906. Her hoard of hard-earned money was growing. She now had her eye on some new real estate investments, perhaps making up for her disappointment that she had missed out on the Klondike gold rush. Mary was among a significant group of immigrant Irish women who astonished everyone with their astute investments, and with the amounts of money they were able to accumulate by running a boardinghouse.

The Camerons had a few more chores to do in town and then left for home. It started to rain as they approached Eve Ranch, but it was pleasant enough for them to eat supper at eight o'clock on the verandah. "Wrote diary. Bed 10.15."

'Although she made no mention of purchasing a large quantity of meat that day, Evelyn noted in her diary entry for the next day: "Meat (fresh) got very dirty yesterday coming up in wagon. Had to wash it, bone it (all stewing pieces) put to stew, bones to soak for

Meetings With Mrs. Collins

Drummond House, Terry, Montana, 1910. Mary Collins operated her boardinghouse here from 1886 to 1898, when Evelyn wrote: "She has sold out for $900 to Mrs. Drummond to be paid in monthly installments of $10. $50 in cash." *Cameron photograph, courtesy of the Prairie County Museum, Terry, Montana. (Box XIX, Neg. 32, EC67)*

stock, some little salted & some into the pickling jar . . ." Lacking refrigeration, Evelyn had learned some frontier preservation techniques. Her 1896 diary records a recipe for meat pickling: "1/4 lb. salt, 1 lb. sugar, 2 oz. saltpeter, 1/2 cup mollasses, 2 gals. water. . . I washed 19 lb. meat & poured this over it, have to leave it 2 weeks (in spring)."

Some of the meat was for their dogs. "So much dog food to cook. . .," Evelyn remarked in her diary.

* * *

THURSDAY, AUGUST 4, 1898
<u>Gathered vegetables. Steel got away. Wagon [to] Terry. Puppies off.</u>
Cool. Bright. Thunder 11.

Colleen Elizabeth Carter

Evelyn arose at 6:10. She took a cold bath, finished her chores, and ate her breakfast alone. The horse Steel had broken through the gate and "footed it to Coil's fence." After retrieving the horse, she "dressed terrific hurry," anxious to get to Terry as soon as possible.

She put four puppies into an Arbuckle box (Arbuckle coffee, "The coffee that won the West," was patented in 1865 by John Arbuckle, after he and his brother Charles developed a process of coating roasted beans to preserve the flavor and aroma. The airtight, one-pound packages were shipped in sturdy wooden crates, one hundred packages to a crate.) She also quickly gathered some of her first cabbages of the season, along with some cucumbers and onions for Alec to sell.

Evelyn hoped to get to the post office as soon as the mail train arrived. There were two letters from Ewen, who had gone to Miles City. Later in the day, a wire arrived saying he would return the next day.

Evelyn took one of the cabbages to Mrs. Collins, who fixed her "milk & oatmeal mush." Mary had some surprising news: "She has sold out for $900 to Mrs. Drumond to be paid in monthly installments of $10. $50 in cash."

This transaction likely marks the end of Mary Collins' boardinghouse days. She would have been sixty-five years old. The story passed down in our family has it that when she retired, the cowboys held a big party for her, and presented her with a "silver-studded saddle." If the story is true, Evelyn does not mention the event in her diary.

On October 17, Mary purchased lot one, in block thirty-nine, on Laundre Avenue, from John Stith, for $225. The long, narrow wood-frame building that stood on the lot, a former store, became her new home.

Mary would continue to take in an occasional boarder. In 1901, the George Burt family would stay there during construction of their large log house in town. According to Donna Lucey, Burt, an engineer by training, and a great innovator, was among the most prominent and successful sheep ranchers and businessmen in that part of the state. In 1905, he would become a state legislator. His daughter Lucille owned the first bicycle in Terry, and he brought

Meetings With Mrs. Collins

the first automobile to the area. In a 1977 letter to Mary Haughian, Lucille fondly recollects living in "Grandma Collins'" house for a short time before moving into their new home. Mary Haughian suspects that Mrs. Collins' grandson Lynn was once in love with Lucille. Evelyn would take many photographs of the Burt family, and their ranching operations.

In 1906, Stith would buy the lot back from Mary for $600. He later rented out the building for performances and "magic lantern" shows. Church services were also held there until Stith built a permanent church. Stith's civic-mindedness was typical of many early frontier businessmen, and did not arise purely from altruistic motives. In those days small towns all along the railroad lines competed with each other to attract new settlers. Stith had learned that the more a town could boast of its "culture" and "civilization," the faster the town, and its businesses, would grow and prosper.

* * *

Evelyn's 1898 diary contains many more contacts with Mrs. Collins:

January 22: "To Mrs. Collins she much better, to Mrs. Stith in bed 1 baby of twins died to day the other I saw very tiny 2 lbs weight. The others navel didn't drop off for five days probably cause of death normally comes off 3 days she says. Wrote to Bach at Collins asking him to try & obtain an Avery pup as he has taken to 2 up there."

February 21: "To see Mrs. Collins Mrs. Burgh there. Mrs. C says I ought not to pay more than $15 for Scott's steel range."

April 3: Went to Collins. She gave me a lot of cookies which E & I ate some of on our homeward way."

April 19: "Borrowed mattress & bed cot from Mrs. Collins." (The Camerons were expecting a visit from their prominent British friend Maj. Dowson.)

May 5: "Counted out 2 settings of 13 eggs each 12 for Mrs. Collins, 24 for Mrs. Atterbury. . . . Left cotts at Collins' & Atterbury's."

June 9: "Got 22# beef from Mrs. Collins 11# of it bone. I

Colleen Elizabeth Carter

hauled 200# tatoes from Depot for her we put them in her wheel barrow to take to cellar last 100 the wheel broke & she exclaimed 'Oh the dam wheel's broke!'"

June 20: "Paid Mrs. Collins $1.20 on meat owe her 1$ more.

July 29: "To Mrs. Collins paid her $1 on meat owed her. Ate doughnut. Gave me some take home."

August 16: "Got 2 bottles Scotts 4 Gipsons, 5 Collins 6 at Butler's on way home. [To bottle wine.] To Collins tea biscuit butter, jelly."

August 21: "Gathered cherries for Mrs. Collins."

* * *

"For a' that and a' that
'Tis comin' yet, for a' that,
That men to men the world o'er
Shall brothers be—an a' that."

—Robert Burns poem, written on title page of Evelyn's 1898 diary.

Chapter 16

"Mrs. Collins has bought the Anderson house and the Jordan barn from Jordan."

THURSDAY, JANUARY 12, 1899
<u>We stayed in camp. Hamlin to get last load of hay. Depart tomorrow.</u>
Dull & strong Westerly wind. Mild. Didn't freeze day. Wind died down at 5.30, but got up again 7.15.

The Camerons awoke at seven forty-five in their tent. They were near the end of an extended winter hunting trip in the badlands, north of the Yellowstone River. Ewen shaved, and Evelyn served breakfast at ten o'clock. They would not leave camp to hunt that day, as they were expecting Mr. Hamlin, their hired hand, to arrive.

When he got into camp at noon, Hamlin urged them to cross the Yellowstone soon. He feared that the mildness of the weather and the westerly wind might mean the arrival of a warm, dry "chinook." He warned: "Old Scott says if there comes with this mild spell a rush of water from the mountains it will buldge the ice up and make it unsafe." The Camerons knew that if the river were to thaw, it could be many days before it would be safe to cross again. "Ewen decided to leave tomorrow & to have Hamlin come & get us across with his sharp shod team & put nails in our s. [shod?] horses."

They had good reason to worry about the chinook—the warm, dry wind named for the Chinook Indians of Oregon, who called them "snow eaters." These strong winds swept down from the eastern Rockies, sometimes creating dramatic weather effects, and great extremes of rapidly warming temperatures.

Evelyn served dinner at one o'clock: "stewed beef, fried kid antelope, cocoa, réchauffée biscuits." Hamlin brought them up to date on the latest news from Terry: "Dead man found on track, believed to be killed by a breaks man though not enough evidence to convict him. Mrs. Collins has bought the Anderson house and Jordan barn from Jordan. The black tan Coil calf is dead at our place."

Mr. Hamlin headed back across the river at two o'clock, and the Camerons spent the rest of the afternoon reading by light from their wood-burning stove. At dusk Ewen went out and "attended osses" while Evelyn brought in water and firewood. She had supper ready at 6:20: "Beef stew, rice, fried kid. Dog ate last of kid antelope today."

* * *

Once again, Evelyn saw fit to record in her diary the real estate dealings of Mrs. Collins. Her new properties, lots three and four, in block thirty-eight, were purchased for $400 on December 23 from her old friends William F. and Mary Jordan, who now owned and operated a hotel in Glendive.

Chapter 17

"First business day in Terry but got no customers."

FRIDAY, JULY 21, 1899
<u>Drove to Terry but no photography. Mrs. Collins</u>
Beautiful. Very hot. 5:50 am 74° 4 pm 92° in Terry

Evelyn arose at five forty-five to distant thunder and a "very inky sky" to the north. The temperature was already seventy-four degrees. She put breakfast on to cook while she milked the cows, cleaned the "fowl house," and fed the chickens. She served breakfast, swept, washed up, and "picked a few service berries." After a quick lunch, she left for Terry. "Took camera with me & screen," she wrote.

By now, Evelyn had become a confident photographer, but demand for her work was growing at a disappointingly slow pace. She photographed Terry residents in their Sunday best in front of their homes, cattlemen at their ranches (sometimes requiring an overnight stay), and sheepherders with their sheep.

By 1899, Terry had become a major center for the sheep-raising industry, thanks largely to John Stith, who had purchased

Colleen Elizabeth Carter

and set up a wool press in town in 1897. Evelyn had hauled her camera and equipment to the shearing sheds in Terry on June 24 to photograph the young men shearing, and took orders for prints, which she delivered two days later. She took many photographs of cowboys, including the legendary XIT cowboys, as they roped and branded cattle, and drove them to the Fallon stockyards.

Evelyn also sold prints of badlands scenes and prairie life as souvenir photos, letting Mrs. Snow sell her prints at the post office for a small commission. That summer, Evelyn photographed Mr. And Mrs. Snow in front of their log home, which also served as post office. They let Evelyn display samples of her work on a sign that she made up on July 4: "Put 6 on the show mount, picture & wrote down the middle Mrs. Cameron. Photographer. 3.00 Per Doz—1.75 Per Half Dozen, 25¢ Each not exceeding four—Please leave orders at Post Office. Winnie B. & her par amour passed & I got them to take it down to Snows."

Evelyn observed in her diary that night: "Ewen not pleased at my having put Photographer on my show photos." Fortunately, she persevered despite her husband's lack of encouragement.

Postmistress Susie Snow and her husband stand in front of the Terry Post Office, where Evelyn Cameron photographed them in the summer of 1899. Mrs. Snow earned a commission for selling Evelyn's photographs. *Cameron photograph, courtesy of the Prairie County Museum, Terry, Montana. (Box XIX, Neg. 15, EC66)*

Meetings With Mrs. Collins

On this sweltering day in Terry, Evelyn ordered, at Gipson's, "enough vaccine for blackleg for 20 head [of cattle]." It was the blackleg disease that would finally defeat Ewen's efforts to raise cattle in Montana. Evelyn's photography business would now be even more crucial to their financial survival, and she would clearly have to work harder to drum up business, and to convince Ewen that the time taken from her ranch and household duties was worthwhile. So far, she hadn't made a cent from her efforts, and on August 4 she would write: "Ewen posted photographic accounts & makes me $4.92 in the hole yet. Made $31. Spent 35.92." Today she had brought her camera to town in hopes of making a sale or two.

When Evelyn picked up her meat at Scott's Terry Hotel, Mrs. Scott made the helpful suggestion that Evelyn would "get more custom" if she were to come to Terry on a regular schedule, one day a week. "Ewen says I can so I shall," she wrote in her diary that night.

She went to see a Mrs. Brackett, a woman with a large family, and "arranged how to take her children one day next week. Chatted on veranda about fruit at Yokohama." Evelyn would attempt to photograph the Brackett children for the next four weeks, but one or the other of them was always sick.

Evelyn thought of photographing Mrs. Collins, but when she arrived late in the afternoon, she roused her from a nap: "She had been lying down & the place was like an oven having been shut up." Mrs. Collins would turn out to be one of her more "particular" subjects, and two months would pass before Evelyn could actually photograph her. Like many proud immigrants who had "made good," Mary wanted this to be more than just her portrait—it would also serve to display her achievements and hard-earned status. She may have thought of sending a copy to her family back in Ireland, if indeed she still had any contact with them. "She wants so much furniture in as well as herself," Evelyn would write.

Evelyn headed home, not having taken a single photograph that day. After supper, and a dessert of gooseberry pie, she got Alec to wash up while she milked the cows. That night there was a "fearful storm of wind & rain."

* * *

Colleen Elizabeth Carter

Laundre Avenue, in Terry, Montana, 1891. When the Camerons arrived, the Scott Family was operating the Terry Hotel, in the foreground. Mary Collins' two-story boardinghouse is at the far left. *Photograph courtesy of the Prairie County Museum, Terry, Montana. (Box VI, Neg. 3, EC44)*

SATURDAY, JULY 22, 1899
<u>Worked up sponge. Down to Terry on Rocket. Put up every Wednesday in Terry notice.</u>
Beautiful only very windy.

Evelyn arose at 6:20 the next morning, delighting in the refreshing aftermath of the night's tempest: "Just beginning to get bright clouds rolling away. Very cool little breeze." She put breakfast on to cook, and quickly fed the chickens and milked the cows. After breakfast, she wiped up the kitchen, and haltered Steel, the horse she planned to ride to Terry that afternoon. She mopped the kitchen and "worked up sponge" for bread.

Her chores out of the way, she went to work preparing her latest photographs: "Pasted 3 photos on mounts. Put up 3, one of Herbert Hamlin on his horse, Myrtle & horse group. Sent to Fallon

Meetings With Mrs. Collins

P.O. with notice I [will be] in Terry Wednesday from 12 to 4."

There was a change of plans at two o'clock, which required her to ride a different horse to Terry. "Expected Mr. Price but he came not. Changed onto Rocket in the pasture." Pursuing her plan to have a "studio" in Terry with regular hours, Evelyn went to the Terry Hotel to rent a room. Mrs. Scott agreed to let her post a sign in the hotel to advertise her schedule. While there, Mrs. Scott introduced her to a sheepherder, Mr. McBean, who complained of the mice and ants in his "summer camp." She made it a point to see Mrs. Collins and Mrs. Brackett to let them know she would "be down every Wednesday." That night she wrote in her diary, "Mrs. B. is going to build a hotel onto her house. 8 bedrooms in it, 2 storys." Before leaving for home, she swung by the post office and "stuck up a notice ... [with] 2 photos by it."

Her supper that night: "Mince, tatoes, tea, popovers." She got to bed at ten fifteen.

* * *

The next Wednesday, July 26, Evelyn got up extremely early, at 4:40, and left for Terry with high expectations. At day's end she wrote across the top of her diary entry: "First business day in Terry but got no customers!" What had seemed such a clever idea had proved to be a flop. After six frustrating weeks, Evelyn was back to making visits around town, trying to find potential customers through personal contacts and word of mouth. This setback must have been all the more galling because she knew that Ewen would be keeping track of each penny spent.

* * *

"To cram a lad's mind with infinite names of things which he never handled, places he never saw, or never will see, statements or facts which he cannot possibly understand, and which must remain merely words to him, is, in my opinion, like loading his stomach with marbles.—James Anthony Froude."

— Clipping glued in the front of Evelyn's 1897 diary.

115

Chapter 18

"Mrs. Ingersol just lost 16 month old baby."

WEDNESDAY, AUGUST 16, 1899
<u>Cooked cherries. Mounted few. Took Scotts garden.</u>
Glorious weather. So bright. Cool

Evelyn woke at 5:20. "Such a perfect morning it was," she wrote. Her chores took her until eight fifteen. Alec, having also gotten up early, was working in the garden, and Ewen was still in bed, so Evelyn ate breakfast alone. She "put berries onto stew," and mounted photographs.

At 12:10, she and Alec left for Terry in the wagon. They went to the post office and saw Mrs. Brackett, who was "not well bowl trouble." They tried to visit Mrs. Collins, but she had "gone to Miles [City] Mrs. Ingersol just lost 16 month old baby." This child, named John, was the second Ingersoll child to die.

Evelyn delivered photographs around town and went to the hotel, where she went down to the Scott's new garden and photographed it: "Looked over the garden fine for first year on fresh turned soil. Took 2 exposures one looking East N.E. & one looking West."

Before heading home, they picked up: "4# salmon from Miss Donovan [Nellie Donovan, depot agent] 10¢ per lb. Loaded up 200# shorts 100# wheat." They stopped at Sophie's, "left a present of vegetables from Alec." That night Evelyn served a supper of "salmon tatoes Etc."

On August 23, when Evelyn showed the Scotts the photos of their garden, they ordered five prints. While in town, she got another salmon, "express from Miss Donovan," for forty cents. Mrs. Collins had returned from Miles City and gave her the latest gossip about Mrs. Mason (who was known to have suffered from serious "heart trouble") and her husband, who the day before were rumored to have "committed suicide in Miles City by taking poison." Today's news was: "Masons are reported to be alive the chlorale [chlorale hydrate, taken for sleep] not having killed them but they took each another dose & result as yet unknown."

* * *

—Books Read '97—
Hypatia – Charles Kingsley January
The White Company – Conan Doyle January
A Gentleman of France – Stanley Neyman Jan.
The Adventures of Sherlock Holmes – Conan Doyle
Under the Red Robe – Stanley Neyman February
The House of the Wolf – Stanley Neyman Feb.
The Exploits of Brigardier Gerarde – Conan Doyle
The Chronicles of Count Antonio – Anthony Hope Jan.
The Indiscretion of the Duchess – A. Hope February
The Memoires of Sherlock Holmes – Conan Doyle
 —Written inside front cover of Evelyn's 1897 diary.

Chapter 19

"Photographed Mrs. Collins"

SATURDAY, SEPTEMBER 30, 1899
Down to Terry. Ewen & I sold 6 hens, 1/2 breed, 50¢ a head. Photographed Mrs. Collins.
Beautiful. Afternoon very hazey. Big fire north side [of Yellowstone River].

Evelyn arose a little before seven o'clock, hoping that the day ahead of her would be more productive than the day before: "Disappointing day," she had written in her diary. "Meant to do so much did so little." Her sleep had been disrupted at two a.m. by a sound of alarm from the chickens, "making their scream of fright." As Ewen and Alec slept peacefully, she rushed out to the hen house, where she found five dead chickens, and the culprit—a skunk. After trying unsuccessfully to kill the skunk with an axe, she got a "16 bore" and shot it, then dragged it to a pit behind a haystack. She then turned her attention to the dead chickens, which she beheaded and hung up. She returned to the house and crawled back into bed, perhaps a bit irritated at Ewen's complaint that she "smelt of skunk."

More frustrations followed. After mounting a number of photographs, and loading a rooster and some chickens into an Arbuckle box to sell in Terry, she and Ewen took off in the wagon. They got no further than the Kempton ranch. Ewen and Mr. Kempton's "long business talk" stretched out to two and a half hours, and it was by then too late to go into Terry. "I was bitterly disappointed," Evelyn wrote, "as I have so much to do before leaving for hunting trip." Ewen was "not very pleased with his Kempton settlements." The evening ended with "cold supper."

Saturday dawned "bright [and] calm." Evelyn loaded the rooster and chickens back into the Arbuckle box and quickly tackled her morning chores. She cut up the chickens killed by the skunk to feed to the dogs, and in the process discovered one more dead chicken that the skunk had "broke the beak of." She also mounted another print, this one for "The Rev. Wagner of Terry."

They left in the wagon at one fifteen. This was the day Evelyn would attempt to photograph Mrs. Collins. She dropped off her camera at Mary's house before she and Ewen did their round of errands. Mrs. Stith agreed to buy all of the chickens except the rooster, but the birds were still in the wagon when Evelyn returned to Mrs. Collins' house.

Mary spent many minutes deciding how to pose herself with her possessions for the most impressive effect, and Evelyn finally "took her after a lot of fuss standing at her door inside & outside also."

Evelyn had just finished, when "Ewen came to say all the chickens had got out of the box. I hurried up & between us we drove them into Mrs. Stith's yard."

Despite her unsuccessful attempt to open a "studio" in July, Evelyn's determination was paying off—business in Terry had decidedly picked up. That afternoon she delivered photos to six customers, and picked up an order for more. Orders were also coming in from Fallon, and she had sent some prints there with Alec the day before.

At eight forty-five that evening, the Camerons sat down to a satisfying meal of "fried chicken, tatoes, butter, pudding."

Meetings With Mrs. Collins

* * *

WEDNESDAY, OCTOBER 4, 1899
<u>Coil called, measured hay. Mounted photos. Down to Terry.</u>
Beautiful day, so calm & bright.

    Evelyn arose at 5:40. Dawn broke with a "red sunrise. Quite cloudless. Little wind." After breakfast and chores, she "set to work mounting about 50 [prints]." The production end of her business—printing, toning, burnishing, and mounting—was beginning to take up a large portion of her day, and had to be sandwiched in between her usual ranching and household chores, as well as the preparations for their upcoming extended hunting trip. Earlier, when she was still learning the craft of photography, she often worked late into the night, losing much sleep in the process. Now that some desperately needed money was coming in, photography began to take center stage.

    Alec was even known to help with kitchen chores, allowing her to begin her photographic work as soon as possible in the morning. The day before she had written, "Hurried through house work as usual. Alec wiped." Ewen was pleased with the added income, and at times Evelyn could count on him to help with the photographic work. She had spent the entire day on her photographs. "It keeps one very busy printing and toning together," she wrote. Today she worked four to five hours mounting the prints, finishing by two fifteen.

    The Camerons left for Terry on horseback, Evelyn mounted on "a crop-eared thing of Coil's, Ewen on Rocket . . ." Evelyn arrived at Mrs. Collins' house with prints of the photographs that she had taken four days earlier. When she showed them to Mary, the response must have been exasperating: "[She] picked many faults out of the photo of her self. She didn't want 6, not good enough, her dress too short, etc, but she thought them very good. I promised to take her again later when [we] returned from hunting trip & *give* her 9 from the plate."

    It's not clear whether Evelyn brought Mary six prints or only showed her samples. It often happened that, after a great deal of

Evelyn Cameron "working on photos." *Cameron photograph, courtesy of the Prairie County Museum, Terry, Montana. (Box XVII, Neg. 405, EC22)*

Meetings With Mrs. Collins

time and labor on Evelyn's part, the client ended up rejecting the prints—Evelyn was only paid for those that were satisfactory to the client. Or it may be, as Janet Stevenson indicates in her "Lady Cameron" presentation, that it was Evelyn who first approached Mary about taking the photographs. This may be why Evelyn emphatically underlined the word "give" when referring to her offer to retake the photos. When Evelyn departed, Mary gave her a "beautiful plain fruitcake."

* * *

The Camerons were about to leave for their yearly hunt on the North Side of the Yellowstone River. They would be alone on this trip—providing a rare opportunity for relaxing, reading, and privacy.

* * *

In Evelyn's 1899 diary, I came across one more contact with Mrs. Collins:

July 3: "To Mrs. Collins sat & chatted . . . Got cookies from Mrs. Collins."

* * *

FRIDAY, JANUARY 12, 1900
<u>Ewen not well but we rode to Terry. Called on friends. Back dark.</u>
Dull. Warm. No wind.

In their camp in the badlands, the Camerons arose at 7:20. Evelyn made breakfast while Ewen "attended horses." She wrote a note to post to Alec, telling him they would return to Eve Ranch on the twenty-third. She also sent a note to Wickham in England, and "signed document for giving authority to him to get all my legal documents from Hussey & Fellows."

Evelyn most likely requested her documents at Ewen's urging. He had repeatedly expressed a desire that they return to England,

and this time Evelyn had consented. Donna Lucey states the reasons for their decision:

> In July of [1900] they left for Great Britain because of Ewen's poor health, the pleas of his mother in England for care and company, and an epidemic of blackleg disease that was threatening the local cattle herds, including their own. They planned to spend at least two years in Britain, but Evelyn could not bear the slow pace of Old World life, nor could she abide Ewen's mother. . . At Evelyn's insistence they returned to Montana in 1901.

They left camp at eleven thirty or twelve o'clock and reached the river by one o'clock. The warm weather concerned them, but they "ventured across" the ice in spite of water along the riverbank. Evelyn got her horse across by putting wire nails in the horse's hooves. "He never slipped," she wrote. In Terry, they ran into Mrs. Collins at the post office. A bit later Mr. Stith and Mr. Hamlin came in, announcing that the "crossing above is broken & river running whole breadth in places. Everyone wondered [if] we could get across."

Ewen had developed a "splitting headache." They saw Mrs. Collins again: "[She] paid me $2 on $3 account at request as Ewen wanted money." To be on the safe side, Hamlin drove out to the river with them and "tested the ice with crowbar. Bernie Kempton says 4 in. will hold up a horse." After they got back to camp, Ewen began to feel worse: "Ewen got very bad fever & ague after cup of tea."

Close to the day they had planned to leave, the weather warmed up even more, and Evelyn remarked that, "Cedar [Creek] was a rushing torrent." They feared they would have to delay their departure until the ice became more solid.

On the twenty-first, they visited a huge petrified tree bridge. So fascinated were they that they decided to try to measure it: "I stuck an end of the rope into the ground with an iron tent pin dropped rest into the gulch [I went] down to gulch took up the rope & climbed up onto the East but of the tree where it enters the bank.

Ewen very old nurseyfied—thought I would fall! I found cut on the sandstone of the tree *A. Backsell 6/7/1883* & again *T. Perrot. 83,* evidently 2 cowboys I cut *E. J. Cameron* [and Eve Ranch brand] *21/1 1900 1899 & 1900.* Back to Ewen. We ate lunch. Measured the rope to where I had knotted it which made the bridge from bank to bank *72 ft across & 15 ft. 6 in 1/2 the circumference* at East base."

By the end of the month, four-degree temperatures made the ice once again safe to cross, however Ewen's headaches and stomach pains had intensified to an unbearable degree. When their food supply ran dangerously low on the twenty-sixth, Evelyn had to leave Ewen in camp while she tracked down a sheepherder. When she found him, he said he could provide her with a butchered lamb if she would return the next day.

The next morning, she reluctantly left Ewen "with sibley burning & lots of wood," as she rode off into a frigid wind: "Rode Rocket along divide twixt Cedar & Cherry [Creeks] most direct route he slipped very much we went right in the teeth of the wind & it was very cold."

Because of the severe weather, the sheepherder had not expected her to come. Evelyn went into his dark cabin, which was lighted only by leaving the door ajar, and "warmed up big cook stove & he went to catch, kill & dress late lamb . . . Promised him a box of cigars . . ."

Evelyn nursed Ewen until they got word that the ice was safe to cross. After returning to Eve Ranch, Ewen was extremely ill for several months. A doctor from Miles City came to see him on February 9, and recommended that he have his appendix removed in Minnesota. "[The doctor] said Ewen had made a turn for the better & if very careful about diet would recover, but might at any time have a severe relapse. Left opium tablets 'Codeina'."

* * *

"*Read war news at intervals to Ewen from Record & Lloyds News. Roberts & Kitchener on way out to Africa. The Ladysmith besiegers repulsed a concerted attack of Boers but afraid Gen. White will have to give in soon if relieving forces don't soon relieve."*

—Evelyn Cameron's diary, January 13, 1900

Chapter 20

"She couldn't find her gown & lost her false teeth..."

TUESDAY, MARCH 20, 1900
<u>Down to Terry. Photographed people. Saw Monty Archdale & William Mann.</u>
Lovely day. Mild.

Evelyn arose at six o'clock to a "bright morning. Still. Not a cloud." Ever since Ewen's mysterious illness on their winter hunting trip, Evelyn had been preparing special meals for him at the doctor's suggestion. She kept track of his regimen during the course of the day, using red ink to record the details in her journal. Today's entry reads: "Orange 7 [o'clock]; Tea, bacon, toast, 1 egg 8; Injection, good result 9.15; Sago in mutton broth, cornstarch; Stroll morning & afternoon; Tea, toast, 2 eggs 6.20; cocoa, toast 8.10" She recorded the rest of the day's activities in whatever space remained on the page.

Although Evelyn had promised to retake the photograph of Mrs. Collins after their hunting trip, Ewen's illness must have required her to postpone doing so for several months. But the day had finally arrived:

> I got off at 11. Rode Rocket & carried camera tripod . . . I got to Terry at 12. At 12.30 to Mrs. Collins. [She] had great time getting herself & room ready. She couldn't find her gown & lost her false teeth, she thought her dog had gone off with them. Finally she wished me to go & borrow Mrs. Van Horns [teeth] which I did. She had to take them out & wash them first!! Then they proved too large for her mouth. I found hers under bed coverlid. Took 2 of her: 3 seconds, No. 4 diapragm.

All Mrs. Collins' fussing took up much of the afternoon, but must have given Evelyn an amusing respite from her worries about Ewen's health, and their ongoing financial woes. Sadly, it seemed that just as her photographic business was getting off the ground, they would have to leave Montana. On March 12, Evelyn had inquired at the depot about the first class fare to New York—it was $58.85.

Evelyn tried to take more photographs that afternoon at the Snow's, including shots of Mr. and Mrs. Snow, and "2 of Mrs. Drummond's baby girl, 1/2 seconds, 4 diapragm, too dark I am afraid inside Snow's parlor."

Returning home at six o'clock, she found that Ewen had "heated up his midday meal himself." She "worked up sponge at 8.30" before retiring for the night.

* * *

SATURDAY, MARCH 31, 1900
<u>Down to Terry. Photographed Horne's baby again. Tea Mrs. Collins.</u>
Early morning heard first <u>Meadow Lark</u>.
Beautiful, so mild & bright.

Evelyn arose at six fifteen. Before beginning her usual chores, she "stitched skirt," and after breakfast she made bread dough with "flour & whole wheat." At eleven thirty, she rode off to Terry, taking with her the "camera tripod with sack of mutton." She sold the meat in town: "Mrs Coil bought 7# [at] 12¢ = 85¢. Sold rest to Gipson 7# [for] 85¢, Miss Donovan 2 1/2 & Mrs. Burgh 2 1/2 = 60¢."

She went to Scott's hotel, finding three women in the parlor: "Mrs. Braley, Gracie McGil & Miss Bow." Evelyn had brought with her a selection of prints for sale, many of them showing weirdly spectacular scenes of the badlands. Evelyn's personal preferences and interests, however, often ran counter to the prevailing tastes of the local ladies. After looking at Evelyn's prints, Miss Bow "would take only Minnie's [Mrs. Gipson's] car with Mrs. Whipple [and] Mrs. Kempton standing by it. Curious woman, preferring this to picturesque ones of northside."

The last visit of the afternoon was to Mrs. Collins. There she photographed Mrs. Van Horne's baby, "bay window in front of it." Evelyn accepted Mary's offer of tea afterward.

She returned to the ranch at six o'clock and prepared a "cold supper." Ewen was still on his bland diet, which she recorded at the bottom of the page: "2 eggs, cocoa, toast. For his dinner, cornstarch, sago in mutton broth."

* * *

Also recorded in Evelyn's March 1900 diary was this contact with Mrs. Collins:

March 12: "Cut & washed 2 hindquarters of fawn for Mrs. Collins & Mrs. Gipson . . . To Mrs. Collins [she] gave me more bread. Mrs. Gipson there she is better."

Chapter 21

"Off at last... Goodbyes to friends."

APRIL-JULY 1900

The month of April passed with only a few brief mentions of Mrs. Collins in Evelyn's diary:

April 5: "50# tatoes to Mrs. Collins."

April 11: "Mrs. Collins couldn't eat Alec's tatoes & he took them back."

April 28: "Mounted 9 prints for Alec to take down [to Terry]." [She noted that some of the prints were for Mrs. Collins, although none of them appear to have survived in our family. In an e-mail to me dated April 14, 2003, Donna Lucey speculates on the fate of the glass negatives and prints: "Unfortunately, I do not think the photos of Mary Collins taken by Evelyn still survive. Evelyn and her husband returned to England in 1900 (not long after Evelyn photographed Mary) and stayed for a year; she brought with her a trunk of her negatives—and alas, they were lost in England during World War I. I suspect that Mary's image may have been amongst them."

May 24: "Met Mrs. Collins & Mrs. Kempton driving to Terry. Mrs. Collins bought 2 motherless colts from Mrs. Kempton."

* * *

SATURDAY, JULY 7, 1900
<u>Terry in wagon took tents, plum jam, Etc. Home 6</u>
Morn cloudy. Afternoon bright. Windy

Evelyn arose at 6:10, after what had been a difficult night: "Ewen in pain last night, about the bowels & didn't sleep well." Evelyn went out and gathered peas, beans, and onions for Mrs. Van Horne & Mrs. Collins.

Preparations for their return to England were well under way. They left at twelve thirty with a wagonload of their belongings to sell in town. Their camp tents they left at the post office for Snow to sell. The Scotts bought tablecloths, sheets, pillowslips, and napkins. Mrs. Burg bought a "4 gal crock 2 gals plum butter in it . . ." The Brights and Stiths bought fifteen chickens.

Back home, Evelyn opened her mail and found a letter from Ewen's sister: "Letter from Jessie so glad we are going home."

* * *

FRIDAY, JULY 20, 1900
<u>Off at last. Dinner at Hamlin's. Goodbyes to friends.</u>
Beautiful day. Warm. Cool breeze.

Evelyn arose at six o'clock, having had only three hours of sleep: "Ewen stood the bustle very well considering and he groaned most of the night," she wrote. "I couldn't sleep anyhow till 3 am." The reality of their departure was slowly sinking in. She had awakened to an amazing sensation: "No cow, no chicks to feed & milk."

They had finished packing the day before. Neighboring ranchers had come to say "adieu": the Kemptons, Hamlins, Tuslers, and Coils. Evelyn gave away four sacks of old clothes. Today Mrs.

Meetings With Mrs. Collins

In front of Scott's Terry Hotel, left to right: Eunice Gipson, Mrs. Sarah Gipson, Nellie Donovan (depot agent), Laura Thompson, Mrs. George Gipson, Mrs. Henry Scott, Marion Scott, Cady Scott, Ed Hare (on floor), Henry Scott. In 1901, Evelyn wrote, "[Mrs. Collins'] experiences with Miss Donovan as a boarder were very amusing." *Cameron photograph, courtesy of the Prairie County Museum, Terry, Montana. (Box IX, Neg. 49, EC45)*

Tusler returned "& brought photo of herself & Henry that I wished for. Gave her 2 gal. jug of wine to carry back. She could hardly do it." The Drummonds came to pick up some items they had bought earlier.

At eleven forty-five, they locked up the house and set off with both buggy and wagon full of their baggage. They stopped at the Hamlin's for dinner, "cooked in one house ate in t'other very good dinner & so nicely served." They were sad to leave "old Steel," their horse, in Hamlin's pasture.

They arrived in Terry at three o'clock, and took their bags to the depot, some to be checked and some to be sent by freight. "Ours was well within the limit being 295#. 150# allowed on each ticket." They said goodbye to their friends—Mr. Coil, the Kemptons, Mrs. L. Hamlin, Mrs. Bracket, Miss Donovan, Mrs. Gipson.

"H [Henry Tusler] gave me a pair of very pretty gold links & shed tears at parting. Had to get cake from Mrs. Collins. She would insist Alec had stolen an orange from her a few days ago!"

They got to bed at 10:20 in a room at the Terry Hotel. Tomorrow they would leave by train for New York City, the first link in their return to England.

* * *

The 1900 census for Terry Precinct gave Mary Collins' age as sixty-three, born March 1837, divorced, with four children, three living. She had not yet become a U.S. citizen, but could read, write, and speak English. She owned a house, free of mortgage. Her daughter Rose was listed in the Miles City census, married to stock raiser George Ingersoll, with two children, Lynn and Dixie, and two deceased children.

Chapter 22

"General Miles hitched onto our train in a private car."

WEDNESDAY, SEPTEMBER 4, 1901
<u>Up to Kemptons. Mrs. Collins</u>
Fine, rather hot.

More than a year passed before Ewen and Evelyn returned to Terry. They awoke in the Scott's Terry Hotel, having just returned from their lengthy stay in England. The day before, as their train rolled through North Dakota, they had watched the countryside pass by and ate from their fruit basket. At one o'clock they pulled into Bismarck: "Rather nice looking American lady sat next to us. Dinner 6. General Miles hitched onto our train in a private car. [General Miles had recently put in an appearance at the Pan-American Exposition in Buffalo.] I saw his baggage in the baggage car & 3 pointers. Arri. Terry 10, 2 hrs. late. Fearful long train. Got off far from depot. Mrs. Scott, senior, K. Scott, met us." She had noted in her diary that night: "Hotel changed old saloon on east side turned into kitchen & dining room."

They ate breakfast at eight o'clock, straightened their room, and went out in search of old friends. After seeing Stith and Gipson, they went to Mrs. Collins' house. "She was wheeling barrow of coal. Sat in her parlor & chatted. Her experiences with Miss Donovan as a boarder were very amusing. Miss Donovan gone some time ago. Man named Rippon here now as R.R. agent."

Ewen lay down after lunch, exhausted from the long journey. They started for the Kemptons at three o'clock. On the way, they saw Mr. Hamlin, Sr., in his buggy: "Hamlin's illness is from the rupture has spells of great pain in the bowels." The Kemptons were glad to see them: "Mrs. Kempton very hearty." They stayed for supper and from the Kemptons heard the rumor that "Mr. Price is going to England with car load of horses." The Boer War had made selling Montana horses very lucrative again, much to Ewen's chagrin.

A number of their Terry friends had gone to Buffalo to see the Pan-American Exposition. It was there, two days later, that a twenty-eight-year-old anarchist named Leon Czolgosz would shoot President McKinley. The next day Evelyn would write: "McKinley not killed hopes of his recovery, one bullet lodged in the muscles of the back other extracted from stomach."

The Camerons soon found a temporary place to live for the eight months they estimated it would take to establish a new ranch on the north side of the Yellowstone River. They rented the Joubert house, about a mile east of town, just south of Mrs. Collins' former homestead. On the eighth, they again went to see Mrs. Collins: "She of course said we had paid too much for the Joubert's place $6 per month altho' no one else thinks so. Donald McDonald was going to give the same rent but quarreled with Joubert over something else & quit the whole thing took the old Locke place close to town."

By the eleventh, they were ready to move out of the hotel. They got their luggage together in the hotel sitting room and went to pay a visit to Mrs. Van Horne, who, they had learned, was the owner of the stove in the Joubert house. At their request, she agreed to let the Camerons use it during their stay. She also told them about a problem she was having with Mrs. Collins: "[She] gives her lots of grief swearing at the children about 20 lambs they are keeping now."

After dinner, men came with a wagon and loaded their belongings, along with a supply of groceries, hardware, and "bread & eggs from Collins. Quite a load. Cady [Scott] came on behind us with wood & coal (Fargo coal). Helped unload the heavy things & I help with coal. Put things to rights a bit. Corrals & out buildings very dilapidated."

Evelyn cooked up a supper of "fried bacon, boiled eggs, toast and tea," and went to bed at ten o'clock. "Very weary on legs," she confessed. Moving into the house would keep Evelyn occupied for weeks, unpacking their boxes and trunks, and dealing with piles of rubbish, "bugs galore" (requiring a sulphur fumigation), and mice.

On September 13, the Camerons, unable to round up the horses to pull their wagon, were forced to walk to Terry, carrying a quarter of a sheep. They gave some to Mrs. Collins ("Left Mrs. Collins a little mutton."), and the rest to the Scotts. The latest newspaper contained the sad news: "McKinley became unconscious 8 morning & died later. Hope not true." Mrs. Collins had somehow acquired a bird for Ewen's collection. She gave him a dead "rail (bird) . . . was [a] Carolina Crake."

On the fourteenth, they drove the wagon to town to pick up their mail. "Mrs. Collins told us McKinley died yesterday evening at 8 pm." They then returned to their old ranch to see what they could salvage, getting "wetted" by a sudden rainstorm. The place was "in an *awful mess,*" she wrote, but they managed to find some useful items. They loaded up *"2 tables, 1 bedstead mattress & springs, 1 tub, 12 pint mould, 2 baking pans,"* as well as some cucumbers, watermelon, tomatoes and squashes from the old neglected garden. Evelyn confessed in her diary: "Glad [we] don't live up in the hills here now."

Mrs. Collins kept the Camerons supplied with bread while they were settling in. On the seventeenth, Drummond dropped off "bread galore" from Mary.

Evelyn recorded a visit to Mrs. Collins on October 5, and on October 11 she reported a visit from Mary: "Mrs. Collins arrived 2.30 been looking for her cow. I went on Croppie & investigated two bunches without success. Had tea bread butter. She left 5."

Colleen Elizabeth Carter

When the Camerons rode to Terry on Christmas day, Evelyn went to visit Mrs. Collins, taking her "a piece of our plum pudding. She sent me a 'jelly cake' by Mrs. Gibbs [this] morning. We chatted, [she] is cut up about dogs being killed while she was in Miles for a month. Ewen came in talk on rockers." The Camerons seem to have greatly admired Mary's rocking chairs, and would later convince her to part with one.

* * *

"Kitten in house all day & last night did its little besoins dans un boîte dan la quelle il y avait de terre." [Kitten in house all day & did its little "needs" in a box containing soil.]
—Evelyn Cameron's diary, September 18, 1901

Chapter 23

"Mrs. Collins hove in sight 11.20."

FRIDAY, MAY 9, 1902
<u>Mrs. Collins to dinner. Cow hunting. Ewen & I rode looked at Will Coil's homestead. Got 8 Sage hens eggs.</u>
Beautiful. Heavy shower night.

Evelyn arose at 6:40. She had worked hard the day before, indoors and out, and noted: "Too weary a feeling today." She may have been too exhausted to fully appreciate her unexpected visitor: "Mrs. Collins hove in sight [at] 11.20. She came in was cow hunting. She gave me a long harangue about Stith. Miles City merchants she maintains are just using him (Chairman of Board of Supply) to further their own ends viz: facilitate by every means possible, without regard to taxpayers interests to the furtherance of their trade by building Yellowstone bridge school ... [illegible] High to be built Etc. Stith being green is swayed by the board to suit their own purposes & all County people are now up in arms against him. He is now on a trip inspecting roads leading to Terry with view of improving same for benefit of his trade!"

During this outburst, Evelyn prepared a dinner of "boiled ham croquettes, mashed potatoes, prunes. Large batch of oat cake." Evelyn noted in her diary that, "Mrs. C. had a glass of beer which she affirmed gave her the tisie."

B. Stith's book, *Terry Does Exist*, sheds some light on Mary's "harangue." In 1900, John Stith had been elected to the board of Custer County Commissioners, a position that required much of his time and energy. During his tenure the first Yellowstone Bridge at Terry was built, requiring the hiring and overseeing of work crews, teams, and wagons. He often went out in a horse and buggy to inspect roadwork. Since the local property owners shouldered the burden of the "road tax," Mary apparently did not support these improvements.

Later that afternoon, the Camerons looked at the Coil homestead claim with a view to buying it for their new ranch. They returned home at 6:40.

* * *

Living so close to Terry, Evelyn began to visit the town more frequently. Mentions of Mrs. Collins in the diaries decreased, however. Perhaps most of their meetings were now more casual, and less newsworthy.

That summer, the Camerons purchased their new ranch on the "North Side" of the Yellowstone River, which they also named Eve Ranch. Ewen spent much time there, and by September was getting advice on building sites and well drilling from Mr. Kempton and Reno Walters.

Meanwhile, Evelyn worked hard to revive her photography business. On September 21, Evelyn delivered some prints to people in Terry and, "gave Mrs. Collins [the] Coronation no. of Field [magazine]." (This refers to the coronation of King Edward the VII and Queen Alexandra at Westminster Abbey on August 9.)

The Camerons soon moved out to their new ranch, living in a tent until their house was finished. On December 22, on a day "just cold enough to make ears tingle," they went to Terry for supplies, Ewen in the wagon, and Evelyn riding her horse, crossing the river on the ice. At Mrs. Collins' they had "tea cake bread & butter." Evelyn noted admiringly that she had "got some new arm chairs rockers." The following day, the temperature dropped to fifteen or twenty below, with a "dreadful cold wind," but they were finally able to move out of the tent into their new house.

After the move to the North Side, the Cameron's visits to Terry became less frequent, especially during winter months—and more rushed, as they usually had a long list of supplies to purchase. On Friday, April 24, 1903, they carried home an oak rocker that Ewen had bought from Mrs. Collins for eight dollars. Mary is mentioned only one more time that year—on June 24, when Evelyn talked to her in the Terry post office.

In 1904, Evelyn started writing in a new style of diary. This one required her to cram two day's worth of her life onto one page, so she no longer itemized her daily chores as before. Here are a few entries that mention Mary Collins:

May 28: "Got Mrs. Collins to take Starlight's calf $5." (In April, Evelyn had enlisted a reluctant Ewen to help her pull the calf out of its mother: "To barn, found Starlight . . . [with] her calf's head and fore feet appearing. I pulled and pulled. Ewen *had* to help & we got it out only attached by umbellical cord. It would have suffocated if we hadn't drawn it out, the vagina compressed its lungs so.")

July 11: "Mrs. Collins. Hurried tea"

October 20: "Gave Mrs. Collins little . . . [illegible] Sold 48 eggs."

November 15: "Mrs. Collins ill last night."

November 20: "I called on Mrs. Collins she has been very bad with oppression on lungs."

Evelyn's 1905 diary was even smaller—half the size of her previous diaries. As a result, the writing became even more cramped and crowded. There was only one mention of Mrs. Collins that year. On March 20, she mentions that she "spoke to Mrs. Collins & Mamie." (Mamie Auten was Mary's daughter from Minnesota.)

The 1906 diary also has one mention for the entire year. On February 14, Evelyn "called on Mrs. Collins."

Colleen Elizabeth Carter

1907 was a busy year for the Camerons—trips to Terry were few, and there were no references to Mrs. Collins.

* * *

During these later years, Mary Collins was forced to relive painful memories from her past—the life she had run away from in Minnesota. Her husband Patrick had died on July 8, 1903 of liver and kidney disease in the Minnesota State Soldier's Home in Minneapolis. (He was buried in St. Mary's Cemetery.) Mary may have learned of it in 1905 during the visit of her daughter Mamie, which was mentioned in Evelyn's diary. Knowing that she was eligible for a widow's pension, she journeyed back to Minnesota to present her claim to the Pension Office. It's likely she also returned to reaffirm her ownership of the High Forest property, for she represented herself as a resident and property owner there, with a postal address in Grand Meadow, Minnesota, the small village to the south where she had lived before leaving for Montana. On September 30, 1905, she signed an affidavit claiming her right to the pension. The document states:

> That she is the widow of the above named soldier Patrick Collins and that she was married to said soldier on the 5th day of January 1856 at Union Springs, State of New York by a Catholic priest named John O. Donnely. That her maiden name was Mary-Bridget McMahon.
> Affiant further says on oath that neither she or the said Patrick Collins had been married previous to their said marriage on the 5th day of January 1856.
> That said soldier deserted this claimant on or about the year 1870 and since said year 1870 and up to the time of his death in July 1903 neglected and refused to live with or provide for her or his family of children.
> Affiant further says on oath that soldier left no life insurance—That she owns one lot 66 feet wide and 132 feet long in High Forest Minnesota with house theron—House 16 feet by 18 feet two story high built 50 years ago—House and lot worth

$100—That she has not disposed of any real estate since Sept 23rd 1905—That there is no person legally bound to provide for her support—That she owns no bank stock and has no investments—That said soldier Patrick Collins died in the summer of 1903 at the State Soldiers home Minneapolis Minnesota—and that during the years 1903-4-&5 and several years previous thereto he had no real or personal property and was cared for and buried at the expense of the government.

In November, Mary was back in Terry. She persuaded two friends, Snow, the old postmaster, and W. S. Kasper, to make statements regarding the value of her property in Terry as follows:

That they are personally acquainted with Mrs. Mary B. Collins and know that her Real property in Montana consists of two houses and lots in the Village of Terry. The value of the entire property being about Eight hundred dollars ($800) That at the present time she is deriving no income from said property. That the Rental value of same would not exceed One hundred dollars ($100) per annum and further that Mary B. Collins the Claimant is not possessed of any personal property of value in this County and that her annual income aside from her daily labor does not exceed One hundred dollars ($100) This is in my own hand writing.
S. I. Snow

I have read the above affidavit by S. I. Snow and know personally that the statements made theirin are facts. And I fully concur to the same.
This is written in my own hand.
W. S. Kasper

In 1904, Mary had traded properties with George and May McDonald, ending up with lots eleven, twelve, and thirteen in block thirty-nine, on Logan Avenue, adjoining lot one, which she had purchased in 1898 from John Stith. Although she had worked out a financial arrangement when the Drummonds took over her hotel, that property was still in her name until 1906. As the McDonald lots were considered one property at the time it's reasonable to say that she owned two lots, and she did indeed sell them for $825 within the next two years.

* * *

Patrick Collins' original claim for an invalid pension was filed away with his military records, now at the National Archives. The file is the source for much of what we know about Patrick and Mary. His pension claim, dated May 13, 1892, declares that he was "totally unable to earn a support by reason of Piles—disease of the kidneys and disease of his eyes." He gave his post office address as High Forest, Olmsted County, Minnesota. Even after some forty years in America, he had not learned to sign his name, so inscribed an x on the signature line. Patrick's military file contains some additional documents. In 1894 he was still pursuing his pension claim, and a High Forest farmer and former employer, J.D. Farnham, testified on his behalf in an affidavit, stating that:

> He has been intimately acquainted with the above named claimant for *twenty five years* and that said claimant worked for affiant for a number of years as a hired laborer on affiants farm and that he has seen and talked with claimant during said time as often as once a week and to the best of affiants knowledge and belief claimants alleged disabilities, *piles* and *disease of eyes was not caused by vicious habits* = And that by reason of said disabilities claimant has been disabled from the performance of manual labor from the *21st day of May 1892 up to the present time*. That the foregoing statement was written in my presence by Ely Armstrong of High Forest Minnesota March 5th 1894 and from oral statements made by me and that in making such statements he did not use and was not guided nor prompted by any written or printed statement or recital prepared or dictated by any other person and not attached as an exhibit to this testimony.

Meetings With Mrs. Collins

The Bureau of Pensions, following up on Patrick's claim in November 1892, requested his medical records from the War Department. He finally began receiving his pension in 1894. At the time of his admittance to the Minnesota State Soldier's Home in 1898, the Bureau of Pensions in Washington, D.C. asked the local pension agent to fill out a standard form recording Patrick's replies to these questions:

First. Are you married? If so, please state your wife's full name and her maiden name.
Answer. No. Widdower
Second. When, where, and by whom were you married?
Answer. [blank]
Third. What record of marriage exists?
Answer. None. Lost.
Fourth. Were you previously married? If so, please state the name of your former wife and the date and place of her death or divorce.
Answer. Died in Iowa in 1870.
Fifth. Have you any children living? If so, please state their names and the dates of their birth.
Answer. Two. Sadia Born in 1867. Elsa Born in 1878.

This document makes it clear that Patrick had long since repudiated Mary and their three children. As a result, Mary's claim for the widow's pension would be greatly complicated.

* * *

In the fall of 1906, Mary must have been immensely proud to hear that her son James Collins, my great-grandfather, was elected to the North Dakota state legislature. James had arrived in the town of Page in 1888, and the next year was able to bring his wife there by covered wagon from South Dakota. He proved himself to be a man of substance, owning both a farm and an elegant house in town, as well as a livery stable ("J. F. Collins – Horse shoeing and plow work; harness, robes, whips, etc."). In his stable he kept his prize racehorses: "Sylvione," "Hello Bill," "Violet," and "Josephine." It's clear that James, like his sister Rose, had inherited their mother's Irish determination and ambition.

By the fall of 1907, Mary had sold all of her Terry property. It is doubtful that she was receiving the widow's pension she had applied for, because, on September 16, she was forced to file yet another affidavit with the Pension Office. This one seems to have been written with some difficulty, and is in her own spidery handwriting. Stith's name is provided as a "witness," and, strangely, she also felt it appropriate to include the name of her friend, Mr. Snow, although he was by then deceased. The recipients must have found her closing statement amusing:

> I Mary B Collins
> as you want know how many children was 4
> One is Dead there are 3 living which is
> Mary Madore Collins Autin born November 19 1856
> James F Collins born January 7 1863
> Sarah born December 2 1860 and Dead [illeg.] 12 years
> Rose E Collins born January 17 1866 who is now Mrs. George F. Ingersoll of Miles City Montana cattle man and horse Ranch also
> James F. Collins my son of Page Cass Co Nor Dakota
> Mary M Collins Autin of Jackson Minnesota
> Rose E Collins Ingersoll Miles City Montana
> Sarah E Collins Died inn 18 70 2 seventy tow October 13
> All my witnesses are first-class men
> Mr. John W. Stith is chair man of board of county commissioners of Custer County. Mr. Snow now Dead was post master of terry. W S Kasper railroad contrecter on Milwaukee road
> Mr. Brewbecar [Brubaker] is cashier of the Bank of Terry First Nat Bank I guess the Name
> Mr E P Binck was merchant of High Forest for about 30 years
>
> I swear to all that is correct of this
> Mary B Collins

* * *

Meetings With Mrs. Collins

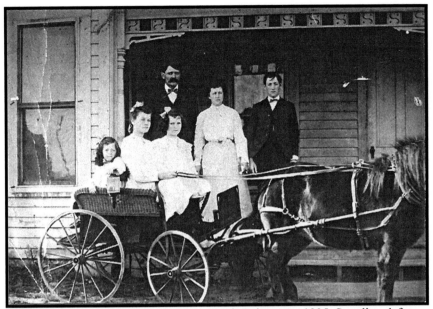

The James F. Collins family, in Page, North Dakota, ca. 1905. Standing, left to right: J. F. Collins, his wife Elizabeth, son William. In wagon, left to right: daughters Jen, Sadie, Lola. James Collins served as a state representative from 1906 to 1909. *Collection of author.*

* * *

"The true moral impulse is directed not so much to the survival of the fittest, as the fitting of as many as possible to survive."
—Written in the front of Evelyn's 1907 diary.

Chapter 24

"Mrs. Collins asked me to stay so did."

WEDNESDAY, AUGUST 12, 1908
<u>Drove to Brights & to Terry. Sold vegetables & 20 chicks.</u>
Cloudy & terribly windy from North.

Evelyn arose at six thirty, did her chores, had breakfast, ironed, and went outside. "Got vegetables from garden: beets beans & cucumbers." With the vegetables loaded into the wagon, along with a box of chicks, she made her way to the Bright's ranch, where they were busy branding. She mentions material for a riding skirt—perhaps Mrs. Bright had agreed to sew it for her.

In 1907, the Camerons had moved once more. Predicting the economic boom that would arrive with the new Milwaukee Railroad, they had bought a new ranch near Fallon Flat, east of Terry, hoping to benefit from the changes that would come.

When Evelyn got to Terry, she sold her chickens for fifty cents apiece at two hotels and at the meat market. Apparently she did not plan to return to the ranch that night: "Mrs. Collins asked me to stay so did." Evelyn did a few more chores in town, and returned for "tea with Mrs. Collins." They went to bed at ten o'clock, likely after a long chat.

The next morning they arose at six o'clock and breakfasted on "canned corn, tomatoes & toast." She noted: "Mrs. Collins feeling well. Got single bill $1."

This must have been Evelyn's first visit to Terry since moving to Fallon Flat, and, apparently, the road had changed. Evelyn, confused by the changes, had to retrace her way before she got onto the new road. She returned with her wagon full of the "stuff" they had stored at the Wrights during their move. She also carried her purchases of cement ($1.50) and oranges ($1.20). It started raining as she got back to their cabin. "Ewen glad to see me."

Trips to Terry from their new home were few and far between. This was Evelyn's only recorded visit with Mrs. Collins in 1908.

* * *

The last Cameron Ranch, Eve Ranch, southeast of Fallon, in winter. It was sometimes called the Marsh Ranch, since it was also near the town of Marsh. *Cameron photograph, courtesy of the Prairie County Museum, Terry, Montana. (Box XI, Neg. 114, EC65)*

Meetings With Mrs. Collins

* * *

<u>Books Read</u>
The Czar's Spy – By William de Queux
The Virginian – By Owen Wister gd.
Dr. Lavender's People – By Margaret Deland gd.
St. Martin's Eve – By Mrs. Henry Wood
"The Gambler" By K. C. Thurston
"The Light of Searthy" by Edgerton Castle
    —Written inside the front cover of Evelyn's 1906 diary.

Chapter 25

Changing Times

TUESDAY, NOVEMBER 9, 1909
Jen, Mabel, Ewen & I rode to Terry. Mabel proved up on her claim. Roy & Jimmy John by freight.
Cloudy. Mild & still.

Evelyn arose at four fifteen, and had breakfast prepared by 5:40. It was still too dark to milk, so she read for a while, then went out to the barn and "milked by lantern." At seven thirty, Ewen set off to a neighboring homestead to pick up two young ladies, Janet Williams, known as "Jen," and her sister Mabel.

The Williams family—father, two girls, and brother Roy—had arrived by train from Minnesota in 1907 and staked homesteading claims close to the Cameron's new ranch near Fallon. The two girls had become frequent visitors. As Donna Lucey explains:

> Janet in particular captivated the Camerons, and she became a kind of surrogate daughter to the childless couple, living a good part of the time at their Eve Ranch. Evelyn and Ewen

taught the sickly young woman from the city how to ride horseback, and took her along on overnight trips herding their cattle and horses. They also tried to teach her French and encouraged her musical talent as a pianist . . . Janet referred fondly to Evelyn as "Madre" and to Ewen as "Mon Pere," and it was Janet who would inherit the Cameron ranch together with all its contents when the widow Evelyn died in 1928.

The day before, Jen had arrived at the ranch in high spirits. Evelyn reported: "Jennie arr. 2.15. wrestled in the kitchen . . . Ewen gave french lesson." Jen left at five o'clock, making arrangements to meet at seven thirty the next morning and "go to Terry [on] horseback for Mabel to prove up [on her homestead]. Ewen is a witness."

Evelyn left for Terry just before nine o'clock and "caught them up on hill going down to Fallon Creek." They got to Terry at noon and ate at the Central Hotel, where they celebrated with a "good pork, apple pie dinner." Roy Williams and a friend named Jimmie John arrived on the train and joined them for the occasion. Evelyn "paid $3 for six dinners." Afterward, Mabel went to the Roylee Store for "flannelette cottons, Etc.," and Evelyn went to pay a Mrs. T. $1.75 for an eight pound turkey.

Evelyn then took Jennie to meet her old friend Mrs. Collins. As usual, Mary did not hesitate to share the latest gossip, nor did she spare the gruesome details: "[She] told us Will Savages wife shot her self with 45 cal. revolver in mouth before a looking glass last Friday."

Following their visit with Mrs. Collins, Evelyn and Jennie joined their companions at the State Bank of Terry. There, Mr. W. A. Brubaker completed the paperwork on Mabel Williams' homestead claim, thus making her an official landowner.

This was the last recorded meeting between Evelyn and Mrs. Collins, for it was not long after that Mary suffered a debilitating stroke. A number of the old-time settlers were passing on, and Evelyn mentions a few of the deaths in her diaries, but I found no mention of Mary's passing.

Meetings With Mrs. Collins

* * *

Earlier that year, an unsettling reminder from Mary's past had returned to trouble her in her last years—and may even have precipitated her demise. The Pension Office had written asking for more information about her marriage to Patrick Collins. It seems that another Mrs. Patrick Collins had surfaced—and she also had claimed the widow's pension. This forced Mary to file yet another affidavit, which was received in the Pension Office on February 4, 1909. The document states:

> That she never applied for or was granted a divorce from the above named soldier. That she is informed and believes that said soldier after he deserted this affiant in 1870 went to Glenco Minnesota and married and was arrested on a charge of bigamy. That affiant saw soldier two or three times after he deserted her but does not know that he had any permanent home. Some of the time he lived with his son James Collins in North Dakota and during the last years of his life he was an inmate of the Soldiers Home Minneapolis Minnesota. Affiant does not know that said soldier ever applied for or procured a divorce and that she does not know where said soldier resided any particular year since 1870. He lived a wandering life until he became an inmate of the Soldiers Home.

In April the Pension Office received a letter from the Dodge County District Court:

> *There is no record of the marriage of Patrick Collins and Monday Wilson in this office.* But there is a record of a John Collins and Amanda Wilson. The names are so similar that I thought perhaps you got the names confused. Am sorry that I did not make it more clear. This John Collins and Amanda Wilson were married at Fair Point, Minn. The 31st day of Dec. 1871. Witness, Mrs. Shaver and David Shaver.

This latest flurry of bureaucratic activity seems to have finally settled once and for all the identity of the real Mrs. Patrick Collins, verifying Mary's right to her husband's military pension.

Mary Bridget Collins died of a cerebral hemorrhage on October 19, 1911. Her obituary in the *Terry Tribune* describes her final two years:

> In the winter of 1909 she was stricken with paralysis, and for weeks it was feared she would not recover. By careful nursing from the daughter, Mrs. Orton [Auten], who came from her home in Minnesota, and friends in Terry, she recovered, but the disease had left the mind impaired and transformed her into a child. A year ago she was taken by Mrs. Orton to her home in Jackson, Minn., where she has since resided.
>
> The best information obtainable places the age of Mrs. Collins at 80 years. She leaves a son and two daughters, one of them the wife of Dick Ingersoll, one of the largest horse ranchers in this section.

Mary's friend John Stith also died that year, in December, a tragic loss to his family, and to the community he had done so much to build up. Had they lived longer, neither he nor Mary would have approved of the changes wrought by the new railroad and the influx of new homesteaders—along with some undesirables. In 1907, a Terry Tribune article had reported: "From a population of about 50 persons 18 months ago, Terry now has, at a low estimate, 350-400 people and is growing fast." By 1910, Terry had become quite a different place, with brothels doing a brisk business northwest of town, and Terry citizens complaining of noise and public drunkenness.

According to her death certificate, Mary's date of birth was March 17, 1833, her age at death, seventy-eight. This accords with the age she gave the Minnesota census taker in 1860. (When she was in her sixties, whether from vanity or forgetfulness, she gave her age as from four to six years younger.) She was buried in the cemetery in High Forest, Minnesota. No stone marks her grave, but most likely her final resting place is next to her beloved daughter Sarah.

Meetings With Mrs. Collins

The final document from Patrick Collins' military file contains the following report to the Commissioner of Pensions:

SIR: I have the honor to report that the above-named pensioner [Mary Collins] who was last paid at $12, to 4" Sept., 1911 has been dropped because of death 19" Oct 1911.
Very respectfully,
J. B. Fuller,
United States Pension Agent.

Mary's grandson, Lynn Ingersoll, would one day marry Bernice Kempton (whose father Berney was a performer in Doc Carver's Wild America show and later the proprietor of the Kempton Hotel in Terry). They would ranch on Custer Creek, near Terry, raising horses descended from stock belonging to Lynn's father, pioneer cattleman George F. Ingersoll.

Unfortunately, the marriage of Lynn and Bernice would not last, and Bernice would raise her four children alone. The children's fragile connection to their Collins ancestor waned. Lynn Ingersoll, in his old age, would return to Terry and share memories of his eccentric grandmother with the Haughians, who had bought his ranch.

The memories of Mary Collins, however, would live on in another of her grandsons, William Collins, my grandfather. Born in 1889, and growing up in Page, North Dakota, he had heard tales of his Irish grandmother and her Montana adventure from his Aunt Rose, and would eventually pass these tales on to his four daughters. The Collins girls never tired of hearing their father talk about "Grandma Collins." His stories connected them to their pioneer heritage, and instilled pride in their ties to "old Oireland."

How excited they would have been had they known that their great-grandmother had also captured the imagination of the pioneer photographer Evelyn Cameron, and that from between the leather-bound covers of her diaries, Mary Collins would, many years later, emerge to take her own place in the history of the American West.

* * *

Mary Collins' grandson, William Collins (1889-1947), on left, with his father-in-law, Richie Moses Pannebaker. Postcard photo taken in Alberta, Canada, dated January 29, 1914. *Collection of author.*

Meetings With Mrs. Collins

* * *

Evelyn Cameron regretted the changes brought by the new century. The ranching era she had loved and documented with her camera was vanishing. The Enlarged Homestead Act of 1909, called the "dryland farm act," increased the land allotment from 160 to 320 acres, and would lead to a new flood of settlers.

In 1909, The *Terry Tribune* reported that: "As a farewell event at the Hachett Ranch, the range headquarters of the XIT outfit, O. C. Cato tendered a barbecue on Oct. 8. The XIT is closing out and by next year will be only a name on the page of Montana range history." As Evelyn wrote to her brother Percy in 1911[he had visited in the early '90s]:

> The range country that you knew so well is about gone now & the prairie swarms with farmers who plough up the land with steam and gasoline engines. The only consolation we have is that they have not begun to plow the badlands although someone may soon invent an effective contrivance for even this.

The arid lands to the south of Fallon, which had never been considered suitable for farming, were now being settled by trainloads of immigrants and American homesteaders, derisively called "Honyockers," who believed that the new, so-called dry farming techniques would cause the prairies to bloom.

In his book *Bad Land*, Jonathan Raban observes that although Evelyn, like most of the old-timers, was outspokenly skeptical, she nevertheless played a role in the railroad's propaganda, unwittingly luring gullible homesteaders to lands that actually, as it turned out, could not support much farming at all. Pamphlets widely distributed by the Milwaukee Railroad now featured photographs taken by Evelyn Cameron. Prospective homesteaders, looking at Evelyn's alluring photographs of industrious farmers tilling rich, productive soil, had no way of knowing that they portrayed the valley lands along the Yellowstone River, and not the poorer lands they would be offered.

Raban's book provides a fascinating study of the corporate and government manipulation that led to the land boom and its collapse in the 1920s, which drove hundreds of disillusioned and disaffected farmers back where they came from, or further west into western Montana, Idaho, and Washington.

Evelyn wrote articles about her early experiences in Montana for magazines in England. She and Ewen collaborated on articles about Montana birds and other wildlife. In 1912 and 1913, the Camerons made two trips to central Montana to study birds. Evelyn's journal entries and the photographs she took on those trips are presented in Henry L. Armstrong's *The Camerons – Evelyn and Ewen: Birding in Central Montana, 1912-13*.

Ewen's health was steadily deteriorating. On February 11, 1914, when it seemed that he would not be able to survive another cold winter, the Camerons left Montana to seek medical help. As they would eventually discover, Ewen had an advanced form of cancer of the liver and brain. Evelyn tried to make him as comfortable as possible in a cottage near the ocean in Long Beach, California, until his death in a Pasadena sanitarium on May 25, 1914. Her good friend Effie Dowson soon arrived, with her four Pekinese dogs, to be at her side.

Evelyn returned to Eve ranch, where she lived alone, but for the close companionship of young Janet Williams, to whom she would eventually bequeath her belongings, including her camera, photo albums, glass-plate negatives, and diaries. She continued to live much as she had lived in the 1890s, eschewing all modern innovations save her camera and her beloved Victrola. She died on December 26, 1928 of appendicitis.

Evelyn Cameron gained national recognition following the 1990 publication of Donna Lucey's *Photographing Montana, 1894-1928: The Life and Work of Evelyn Cameron*. On November 9, 2001, she was inducted into the National Cowgirl Hall of Fame in Fort Worth, Texas, and, in 2005, her life and work became the subject of a Montana PBS documentary, *Evelyn Cameron: Pictures from a Worthy Life*.

* * *

Steam engine used in dry farming. The engine is pulling a tiller, followed by a packing (clod-busting) machine, a harrow, and grain drills to plant the seeds. "This outfit may have belonged to Otis and Sheldon, who lived near Evelyn, and who did custom farming about 1912-1920." (Information from a Prairie County Museum board member.) *Cameron photograph, courtesy of the Prairie County Museum, Terry, Montana. (Box XX, Neg. 45, EC68)*

Conclusion

The stories of real people have great appeal to modern-day Americans, who hunger for tales that connect them to their past. In the telling of America's history, the long lack of women's stories is gradually being rectified, allowing us to take a new measure of the qualities that propelled our ancestors across a continent.

The stories of frontier women reveal their enormous capacity for endurance in the face of change and challenge. We particularly admire their courage—the courage to leave everything behind and set off for an unknown fate in a new land, and the courage to survive the hardships they found there—a courage often born of desperation. In learning more about their lives, we also have the opportunity to take stock of ourselves.

Retelling the stories of people who lived in the past is a complex and subjective task. Looking at the Western experience from today's vantage point, our admiration is tempered by our knowledge of the devastation that was inflicted upon the Native Americans, the buffalo, and the native grasslands. Nonetheless, in reading Evelyn's diaries, it is hard not to be affected by the heroic quality of her early Montana experiences. How extraordinary it is to discover a voice from the past that helps us look beyond the stereotyped images of western women to see how the West was really lived. Evelyn's voice helps us see the frontier in intimate detail, experienced through the eyes of a woman dealing with profound change in her life, negotiating a new role for herself in her marriage, and ultimately finding artistic fulfillment and economic independence.

Colleen Elizabeth Carter

The West's rough new settlements opened the way for the early flowerings of feminism to reach a fuller expression. Although coming from such disparate beginnings, Evelyn Cameron and Mary Collins had the courage, the vigorous constitutions, and the yearning for a new existence that allowed them to be liberated by life on the frontier, not defeated by it.

Both women had unique qualities that inspired the admiration of those who knew them. But, even by frontier standards, they did not really "fit in." Neither woman had the time, or the inclination, to participate in Terry's many cultural and church activities. Denied this social interaction, they appreciated the rare opportunity for female conversation, sharing of ideas, emotional support, and it was this that nurtured their unlikely friendship.

In reading the diaries, I was especially moved by the small kindnesses Evelyn and Mary bestowed upon each other: Evelyn serving and cleaning in Mary's cook tent at the Fallon roundup, making her bed when she was ill with "the grip," even searching her bedroom for the missing false teeth; and Mary's gifts of fruitcake, chickens, an occasional meal, motherly advice, and delightful tales, told with a charming Irish lilt.

My original quest to find a photograph of my great-great-grandmother may never be fulfilled, but the Cameron diaries have given me these intimate images, which speak to me from the past as vividly as any photograph, and it is these images that reveal the true characters of these remarkable women.

Remains of the Cameron's log house at their ranch near Terry, 2005.
Collection of author.

References

Abbott, E. C. ("Teddy Blue") and Helena Huntington Smith. *We Pointed Them North: Recollections of a Cowpuncher.* Norman: University of Oklahoma Press, 1955.

Ambrose, Stephen E. *Nothing Like It in the World.* New York: Simon & Schuster, 2000.

Anderson, Elizabeth Preston. "Under the Prairie Winds."(Fargo: NDIRS, File #653, 1958).

Andrews, Gen. C.C. "Narrative of the Third Regiment." *Minnesota in the Civil and Indian Wars, 1861-1865.* (St. Paul: Board of Commissioners, 1890).

Armitage, Susan and Elizabeth Jameson. *The Women's West.* Norman: University of Oklahoma Press, 1987.

Armstrong, Henry L. *The Camerons, Evelyn and Ewen: Birding in Central Montana: 1912-1913.* [Montana]: Henry L. Armstrong, 2002.

Bartlett, Richard A. *The New Country: A Social History of the American Frontier, 1776-1890.* New York: Oxford University Press, 1974.

Boorstin, Daniel J. *The Americans: The Democratic Experience.* New York: Random House, 1973.

------. *The Americans: The National Experience.* New York: Random House, 1965.

Butruille, Susan G. *Women's Voices from the Western Frontier.* Boise: Tamarack Books, 1995.

Cameron, Evelyn. *Diaries, 1893-1909.* Archival Sources at the

Montana Historical Society, Helena, Montana: *Cameron, Evelyn and Ewen. Manuscript Collection 226.*

Clarke, Norm. *Tracing Terry Trails: A Chronological History Compiled for Terry Country Centennial Celebration.* Assisted by Wynona Breen, Jane Frank. [Montana: s.n.] 1982.

Coleman, Terry. *Going to America.* Baltimore: Genealogical Publishing Co., 1987.

Conlin, Joseph R. *Bacon, Beans and Galantines: Food and Food Ways on the Western Mining Frontier.* Reno and Las Vegas: University of Nevada Press, 1986.

Dary, David. *The Buffalo Book: The Full Saga of the American Animal.* Athens: Swallow Press/Ohio University Press, 1989.

Davis, William C. *The American Frontier: Pioneers, Settlers, and Cowboys, 1800-1899.* Norman: University of Oklahoma Press, 1999.

Dick, Everett. *The Sod-House Frontier, 1854-1890.* New York: D. Appleton-Century Company, 1937.

Diner, Hasia R. *Erin's Daughters in America: Irish Immigrant Women in the Nineteenth Century.* Baltimore and London: The Johns Hopkins University Press, 1983.

Drago, Harry Sinclair. *Great American Cattle Trails: The Story of the Old Cow Paths of the East and the Longhorn Highways of the Plains.* New York: Dodd, Mead & Company, 1965.

Fish, Peter. "Lady With a Camera." *Sunset*, July 2000, 20.

Gordon, Samuel. *Recollections of Old Milestown.* Miles City, Montana: [Independent Printing Co.], 1918.
http://www.milescity.com/history/ebooks/room

Hines, Robert V. and John Mach Faragher. *The American West: A New Interpretive History.* New Haven: Yale University Press, 2000.

Hoopes, Lorman L. *This Last West: Miles City, Montana Territory and Environs, 1876-1886, the People, the Geography, the Incredible History . . .* Helena, Montana: Sky House Publishers, 1990.

Howard, Joseph Kinsey. *Montana, High, Wide, and Handsome.* New Haven: Yale University Press, 1959.

Jameson, Elizabeth and Susan Armitage, eds. *Writing the Range:*

Race, Class, and Culture in the Women's West. Norman: University of Oklahoma Press, 1997.

Jones, Helen Carey. *As We Recall, A Centennial History of Custer County, Montana, 1889-1989.* Dallas, Texas: Curtis Media Corp., 1990.

Laskin, David. *The Children's Blizzard.* New York: Harper Collins, 2004.

Lavender, David. *The Great West.* New York: American Heritage Inc., 1965.

Laxton, Edward. *The Famine Ships: The Irish Exodus to America.* New York: Henry Holt and Co., 1996. Amer. ed. 1997.

"The Legend of Arbuckle Coffee Traders." http://www.arbucklecoffeetraders.com/legend.html

Lewis, Meriwether and William Clark. *The History of the Lewis and Clark Expedition.* Elliot Coues, ed. New York, Dover, original publ. 1893.

Litz, Joyce. *The Montana Frontier: One Woman's West.* Albuquerque: University of New Mexico Press, 2004.

Lucey, Donna. *Photographing Montana, 1894-1928: The Life and Work of Evelyn Cameron.* New York: Knopf, 2000. Missoula, Montana: Mountain Press Publishing Company, 2001.

Luchetti, Cathy. *Home on the Range: A Culinary History of the American West.* New York: Villard Books, 1993.

Lynch, Thomas. *Booking Passage: We Irish and Americans.* New York: Norton, 2005.

McLaird, James D. *Calamity Jane: The Woman and the Legend.* Norman: University of Oklahoma Press, 2005.

Miller, Kerby A. *Emigrants and Exiles: Ireland and the Irish Exodus to North America.* New York, Oxford: Oxford University Press, 1985.

The Official Northern Pacific Railroad Guide for the use of Tourists and Travelers over the Lines of the Northern Pacific Railroad and Its Branches: Containing Descriptions of States, Cities, Towns and Scenery along the Routes of these Allied Systems of Transportation: And Embracing Facts Relating to the History, Resources, Population, Industries, Products and Natural Features of the Great Northwest. St. Paul: W. C. Riley, 1894.

Peavy, Linda and Ursula Smith. *Pioneer Women: The Lives of Women on the Frontier.* Norman: University of Oklahoma Press, 1996.

Pickard, Madge Evelyn and R. Carlyle Buley. *The Midwest Pioneer, His Ills, Cures & Doctors.* New York: Henry Schuman, 1945, 1946.

Potter, George. *To the Golden Door: The Story of the Irish in Ireland and America.* Boston: Little, Brown and Company, 1960.

Prairie County Historical Society. *Wheels across Montana's Prairie.* [Montana]: The Society, 1974.

Prairie County Museum [Terry, Montana]. Bibliographical Research File: *Elbridge Gerry.*

Raban, Jonathan. *Bad Land: An American Romance.* Thorndike, Maine: Thorndike Press, 1996.

Reinhardt, Richard. *Workin' on the Railroad: Reminiscences from the Age of Steam.* Palo Alto: American West Publishing Company, 1970.

Renz, Louis Tuck. *The History of the Northern Pacific Railroad.* Fairfield, Washington: Ye Galleon Press, 1975.

Riegel, Robert E. and Robert G. Athearn. *America Moves West.* New York: Holt, Rinehart and Winston, 1964.

Ross, Nancy Wilson. *Westward the Women.* San Francisco: North Point Press, 1944, 1985.

Seagraves, Anne. *Soiled Doves: Prostitution in the Early West.* Hayden, Idaho: Wesanne Publications, 1994.

Sigerman, Harriet. *Land of Many Hands: Women in the American West.* New York: Oxford University Press, 1997.

Slatta, Richard W. *Cowboys of the Americas.* New Haven: Yale University Press, 1990.

Stith, B. (Beryl). *Terry Does Exist: A History of South Eastern Montana Copied from Old Records.* [Terry, Montana: s.n., 1982] "Reprinted on the occasion of the Terry Country Centennial, 1882-1982."

Storke, Elliot. *The History of Cayuga County, 1789-1879.* Syracuse, New York: D. Mason & Co., 1879.
http://rootsweb.com/~nycayuga/storke/page363

Story of the Great American West. Pleasantville, New York:

Reader's Digest Association, 1977.

"Westward the Course of Empire Takes Its Way (1845-1864)," *The Way West: Episode One,* VHS. Directed by Ric Burns and Lisa Ades. [United States]: Shanachie Entertainment Corp., 1995.

Wishart, David J., ed. *Encyclopedia of the Great Plains.* Lincoln, University of Nebraska, 2004.

Woodham-Smith, Cecil. *The Great Hunger.* New York: Harper & Row, 1962.

About The Author

Colleen Elizabeth Carter has degrees in anthropology and library science from the University of California, Berkeley. She has had careers as a librarian and as a teacher. She lives in Northern California.

CPSIA information can be obtained at www.ICGtesting.com
Printed in the USA
267446BV00002B/411/P